D1634110

GLAMOUR
PHOTOGRAPHY

THE PROPERTY OF
GENARO
GIANNANDREA

GLAMOUR
PHOTOGRAPHY

JON GRAY
TEXT BY JOHN WADE

CHARTWELL
BOOKS, INC.

Published by CHARTWELL BOOKS, Inc.
A division of BOOK SALES, INC.
110 Enterprise Avenue, Secaucus, New Jersey 07094

© Copyright Robert Adkinson Limited 1985.

All rights reserved. No part of this publication may be reproduced or transmitted in any form or by any means, electronic or mechanical, including photocopying, recording or any information storage and retrieval system now known or to be invented without the prior written permission of the copyright owners.

ISBN 0-89009-823-9

Designed and produced by
Robert Adkinson Limited, London
Editorial Director   Clare Howell
Editor   Janet Law
Art Editor   Christine Simmonds
Designer   Roy Williams
Design Assistant   Debbie Williams

Phototypeset by Ashwell Print Services, Norwich

Illustrations originated by
La Cromolito, Milan

Printed and bound in Spain by
Graficromo, Cordoba

CONTENTS

CHAPTER ONE
GLAMOUR BASICS 6
THIS IS GLAMOUR PHOTOGRAPHY 8
THE STUDIO 10
OUTSIDE CHANCES 12
FINDING A MODEL 14
WHAT MAKES A TOP MODEL? 16
STRENGTHS AND WEAKNESSES 18
IT'S THE PICTURE THAT COUNTS 20
TAKE IT AS RED 22
DON'T LOSE THE MODEL 24
PUTTING BACKGROUNDS IN THEIR PLACE 26
THE FANTASY FACTOR 28
UNUSUAL ACCESSORIES 30
SOMETHING SLIGHTLY WICKED 32
INTRODUCING THE BIZARRE 34
SHOOTING WHEN YOU SHOULDN'T 36
DETAILS THAT MAKE THE DIFFERENCE 38
DOING WHAT COMES NATURALLY 40
A STANDING START 42
BODY BEAUTIFUL 44
ARMS AND HANDS 46
SMILE PLEASE 48
MAKE UP FOR THE CAMERA 50
FACING UP TO MAKE-UP 52
PUTTING ON THE STYLE 54

CHAPTER TWO
SUCCESSFUL GLAMOUR PHOTOGRAPHY 56
ONE STEP FURTHER 58
STARTING SIMPLY 62
CHANGING FANTASY INTO REALITY 64
BRINGING THE BACKGROUND FORWARD 66
ONE GIRL, TWO MOODS 68
SOFT FOCUS 70
WATER MAGIC 72
THE GOOD, THE BAD AND THE RIDICULOUS 74
KEEP IT TASTEFUL 76
TAKE TWO GIRLS 78
A TOUCH OF THE UNUSUAL 80
USING DRY ICE 82
WORKING UP A SWEAT 84
SNAKES ALIVE! 86
THE RULES OF COMPOSITION 88
CROPPING FOR EFFECT 90
PICTURE SHAPES 92
A SENSE OF DIRECTION 94
MAKING LIGHT WORK 96

AMATEUR LIGHTING, PROFESSIONAL RESULTS 98
A SIMPLE BACKGROUND 100
LIGHTING THE PROFESSIONAL WAY 102
PROFESSIONALS' PROPS 104
WHICH LIGHT FOR WHAT 106
A SIMPLE SET-UP 108
THE MOBILE STUDIO 110
INSIDE STORY 112
DRAMATIC EFFECTS 114
STUDIO SETS 116
FILM TESTS 118

CHAPTER THREE
THE GLAMOUR PHOTOGRAPHER AT WORK 120
CALENDAR GIRLS 122
ORGANIZING A CALENDAR SHOOT 124
GOING PLACES 126
GETTING THROUGH CUSTOMS 128
THE TAN'S THE THING 130
THE OTHER SIDE OF THE CAMERA 132
SPREADING THE COSTS 134
GETTING A BIT FLASH 136
SHOOTING IN THE FOREST 138
THE SURPRISE ELEMENT 140
CHANGING ANGLES 142
OTHER PEOPLE'S HOUSES 144
ALL ROUND THE HOUSE 146
TRICKS OF THE TRADE 148
WATER, WATER EVERYWHERE 150
MESSING ABOUT IN BOATS 152
ON THE ROCKS 154
THE OTHER TYPE OF EXPOSURE 156
CAMERA CARE 158
A CAUTIONARY TALE 160

CHAPTER FOUR
A GLAMOUR PHOTOGRAPHER'S PORTFOLIO 162
JUST ONE GIRL 164
A TOUCH OF HUMOUR 166
YOU DON'T HAVE TO BE BRILLIANT . . . 168
COMIC CUTS 170
COVER STORY 172
SPECIAL EFFECTS 174
FAVOURITE LOCATIONS 176
BEDROOM SCENES 178
A MODEL MODEL 180
GOING OVER BIG 182
THE BEST TIME OF DAY 184
SIMPLE, SUBTLE AND SEXY 186

INDEX 190

THIS IS GLAMOUR PHOTOGRAPHY

Meet Jon Gray, a top-class professional glamour photographer. His work is in demand the world over, for books and magazines, for posters, but most of all for calendars. He is a master of his art.

But what exactly is that art? What *is* glamour photography, and how does it differ from nude photography? Both take as their principal subject a naked figure, occasionally male but far more often female; each photographs that figure in a variety of poses and settings. But there the similarities end.

True nude photography treats the subject very much as an inanimate object, as one element of an exercise in lighting, composition, form, texture; as part of a landscape maybe, or as a landscape in itself – a record of contours, perspective, highlights and shadows. If the viewer is excited by nude photography, it is in the way that he might be excited by, say, the play of light on the distant hills in a landscape, or the caught moment of an athlete's expression as he breasts the tape. Rarely is nude photography erotic.

Glamour photography, by comparison, is designed from the outset to titillate. Its very *raison d'être* is to generate a certain excitement in the viewer, whether by the blatant sexuality of a pin-up picture, or by the soft sensuality of a more subtle eroticism. Paradoxically, glamour photography may not depict nudity at all. A tightly cropped picture of no more than a girl's face can often convey more

glamour than her totally naked body. A look in the eyes, a pout of the lips, maybe even the way a wisp of hair falls across her features, these are all factors that, in their own way, can contribute to the final atmosphere of glamour.

Jon Gray is a glamour photographer in the truest sense. His pictures, by turn, are exciting, inventive, gentle, even funny. Most of all they are glamorous. They are erotic but with none of the crudity that can so often creep into this type of photography; explicit certainly, but subtly so; naughty but nice. The technique that results in his type of picture relies on much more than merely knowing how to use the right camera, film, lens and lighting. He knows how to choose the right model for the job in hand, how to treat her and how to build a rapport that leads her to give of her very best.

This is the real art of glamour photography, and this is where Jon Gray excels. He is a professional, yet most of his techniques and ways of working are based on a simple approach that can be practised and perfected by any amateur photographer. If that sounds like you, or if you already have some experience but want to brush up on your technique, this book will be invaluable. Within its pages you'll find hints and tips, techniques and trade secrets, all revealed by Jon Gray to help you on the road to success. Following his advice will make you a better glamour photographer.

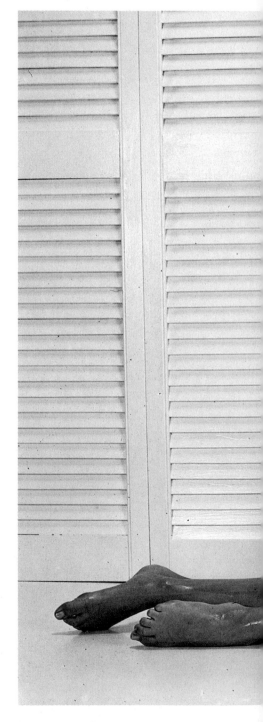

Glamour photography, as opposed to true nude photography, is intended to titillate. It's an art at which Jon Gray excels.

THIS IS GLAMOUR PHOTOGRAPHY

A model's time is precious and, when you are on a tight budget, expensive too. So preparations for a session must start long before she arrives at the studio: sets must be built, lighting arranged, camera angles carefully chosen.

Sometimes a set consists of nothing more complicated than a large, leather sofa before a plain background; at other times a more ambitious background is constructed. A few plants on loan from a local florist, together with some dry ice will produce a dense, steamy jungle in no more than a few square feet of studio space. Bringing in an exercise machine transforms the set into a gymnasium. A few bales of hay with suitable riding accessories suggests a stable.

Jon has his own studio and so has time to build sets and arrange props in advance. If you are hiring someone else's studio, you should first look at it to see what props and equipment are available and what, if anything, you need to bring with you to the session. Always book the studio for at least an hour before the model is due to arrive. This will give you time to make preparations.

The professional glamour photographer always works with an assistant and it's a good idea for the amateur to work the same way. In the studio, an assistant not only moves the lights and changes the film in the camera, he can also stand in for the model before the session, so that the photographer can see the effect of different lights and camera angles.

When Jon goes into a studio session, he does so with very definite ideas about what he wants to achieve. Do the same. Make a list of the items you require as props and the sort of poses you will be photographing. Brief your model in advance, too. Tell her the sort of thing that you have in mind and explain what sort of clothes she should bring to the session. Arrange the set and the lighting in advance. When the model walks into position, made-up and in the right clothes, all the technical details should already have been sorted out and dealt with.

You are free then to concentrate on the most important aspect of all – getting the pose and expression right; making the most of your model and using her precious time to the best advantage.

Sets don't have to be complicated to be effective. Here, nothing more than ordinary studio background paper has been used, together with a couple of palm fronds, to give the picture its atmosphere.

A slightly more ambitious set has been used here, but one that was simplicity itself to construct, consisting of no more than a few bamboo poles strung together in front of studio background paper and, again, with the palm fronds added.

THE STUDIO

OUTSIDE CHANCES

Away from the studio and on location, Jon Gray knows he must still plan his pictures in advance. By the time his models arrive at a location for a calendar shoot, Jon and his assistant will already have been there for a few days, searching the area for suitable backgrounds. Some will be exotic, others might be less so.

In places like Spain or Jamaica, Jon will be looking for locations that could range from houses with ornate exteriors to banana plantations, from the harshness of jagged rocks against thundering seas, to the softness of a smooth, white beach. The practised eye of the professional glamour photographer will also find locations in more ordinary places, like the symmetrically-tiled sides of a half-empty swimming pool, or a plain wall dappled by unusual patterns made by the sun shining through nearby trees.

Light changes in direction, intensity and even colour during the course of a day, so, picking a location in advance, the photographer must anticipate the time at which it will be best lit.

A location must be accessible, easy to get to for both the model and cameraman loaded down with equipment. Privacy is also a prime factor. Some of the best potential locations have to be ruled out simply because the photographer would not be able to work without interruption from crowds of people. Private land is the answer, but permission must always be sought in advance. The photographer should also check the local law. Many countries, whose climate and scenery are ideal for glamour photography, have police who react violently against any form of public nudity. What started out as a promising session can all too easily end up as a night in jail for photographer and model alike!

In the studio, the photographer has all the elements under his control. On location, he must be adaptable. Even in the traditionally sunny tropics, the weather can change unexpectedly for the worse. Faced with a bout of bad weather, the professional glamour photographer will be ready to visit a location that doesn't rely on the sun for its effect. Likewise, the sudden possibility of a dramatic sunset will prompt him to take his models and his gear to just the right place to make the most of the moment.

Preparing for the best and the worst conditions, finding the most photogenic locations, being in the right place at the right time . . . they all add up to successful glamour photography.

Backgrounds like this one are rarely planned back in England. Rather, they are found by the photographer during the first few days at the location and then used when he knows that the time and the light is right.

OUTSIDE CHANCES

FINDING A MODEL

Professional photographers invariably use professional models. They offer many advantages.

A professional model will know exactly what is expected of her. She will know how to pose, the sort of make-up to wear, her best angles, how to arrange her hair . . . everything that she personally can contribute to the shoot.

There are also disadvantages. The very fact that she does know so much about herself and has so much experience often results in set poses, adopted a million times before, simply because she knows they look good. The result on film, however, can lack the originality and sparkle that good glamour photography constantly requires. Also it is very easy for a top girl to be seen around too much. Suddenly her face is on every magazine cover, her body on every calendar.

The glamour photographer, always thinking about a different type of picture, is constantly on the look-out for new faces. And that, sometimes, is where the amateur model comes in.

A girl might send Jon some simple snapshots of herself taken by a friend, and his practised eye will see a potential that might easily have been missed by others. Eager to find a new face, he might invite her to his studio for some test shots and, if they work out, he will take her on to a professional shoot and real work. Posing her will be more difficult than posing a professional but *because* she doesn't know the stereotyped poses, the session will often take on a spontaneity that results in pictures quite different from any that would have been provided by a more experienced girl.

An amateur model has to be very special to be used by Jon Gray for his top work, but, given the right face, figure and eagerness to learn the ropes, she can make it to the top. After all, today's amateur is tomorrow's professional.

A professional model knows exactly what the photographer is trying to convey in any situation and very often can add her own ideas to a pose.

A professional photographer will rarely work with amateur models on location. The long hours and the need to work fast in different changes of light call for the exceptional talents of top-class professionals.

FINDING A MODEL

WHAT MAKES A TOP MODEL?

When Jon Gray interviews models for any assignment he looks for three basic attributes: experience, fitness and personality. Each plays its part in the success of a shoot, and each can just as easily lead to problems. The difference between working with a girl for a few hours in the studio and taking her away to a foreign country for a fortnight's intensive work is considerable.

Shooting a calendar abroad is a lot more difficult than it might at first seem. The model must be capable of giving her all, often in unusual and sometimes uncomfortable locations; spectators might be hanging around; speed can be of the essence as light changes and fades. In all these situations, she must be able to cut herself off from surrounding distractions, to work in a small, private world that contains just her and the photographer. That's one place where experience counts.

Experience is important, too, in the model's knowledge of herself. She will know if she has any imperfections which need to be hidden or which will go against her in certain types of shot, and she must be prepared to tell the photographer any such details at the interview. Jon tells the story of one girl who had everything going for her in the interview, looked fabulous in some test Polaroids, but, once away on location, was discovered to have a scar under her arm, restricting the types of poses she could adopt. A model with more experience would have mentioned the problem at the initial interview.

Some models are much fitter than others. That too plays its part in the pictures. During the first few days of a trip, while the photographer looks for locations, the models make their own preparations. Some spend time working out in a gym. The girls who exercise this way usually make the best models. They know the importance of keeping their bodies in shape. Flat stomachs and firm breasts are as much a stock in trade to them as camera and film are to the photographer. And, in Jon's experience, the old saying 'healthy body, healthy mind' is all too true. The girl who sets out to keep herself fit usually makes a better model all round, showing more interest in the results, giving a measure of her own ideas to the shoot, which all leads in the end to better and more successful pictures.

Location shooting throws people together for relatively short periods that are intensively creative, inventive and productive. That's where personality comes in. The girls chosen for an assignment must be able to get on with each other, as well as with the photographer, the client and anyone else in the group, all of whom know they have only a short time together to get top results. Personality plays its part in posing too. A girl with a naturally effervescent nature can bring a sparkle to a pose that might be lacking in a less outward-going girl.

There are a lot of models, but only a few really *top* models. That's why, despite there being so many different girls on the books of so many different agencies, the same faces tend to crop up time and time again. These are the faces of the professionals, the girls who have learned the golden rules of modelling and who know how to apply them. These are the models at the top of their profession – and they are the girls who are chosen by photographers like Jon Gray time and time again.

Looks naturally play an important role in the choice of a model for a location shoot. But personality is also a major factor, as is good physical fitness.

WHAT MAKES A TOP MODEL?

GLAMOUR BASICS

STRENGTHS AND WEAKNESSES

A model's face and her body are her fortune. However much her personality might contribute to a pose, it's her physical attributes that shine through in the finished product. Looking a model over for her good and bad points, Jon Gray has been known to comment that at times he feels more like a doctor than a photographer.

A firm body is a must. It can even win out over a model's facial looks. Without make-up some models look disappointingly plain. A good face is one that takes make-up well and is transformed by it. A pretty girl has an obvious advantage at the start, but a slightly less pretty girl with the right type of body might just as easily be used for long shots in which her face plays a less important role in the overall picture. Glamour photography is about fantasy;

sagging breasts and flabby stomachs have no place in it.

Hair colour is important. Shooting for calendars will mean using at least two girls, and the client nearly always wants a contrast. So combinations of blondes and brunettes will be put together for a specific shoot. Length of hair also plays its part. The preference is for girls with long hair: when it's long, it can always be made to look shorter, short hair can't be lengthened. A professional model will try to keep her hair as long as possible for that very reason.

A good professional model can stay at the top for only a short while. The girls start to work as early as seventeen years old and by the time they are twenty-four all but a very few special girls reach and pass their peak.

Other, smaller, but none the less important details play a vital part in the choice of a model. Most people have some kind of fear or phobia and, according to the shoot and the type of pictures being planned, the photographer must ask such seemingly inconsequential questions as, is she afraid of insects/water/heat/heights, or does she have any other particular phobia? There is little point in hiring a girl who looks perfect in every respect for a shoot that involves a lot of work on boats, only to find that she has a very real fear of water.

A professional model will not be afraid to mention such things at her interview. She knows her own strengths and weaknesses. Exploiting the former and playing down the latter is what keeps her at the top of her profession.

Long hair can always be made to look shorter than it actually is, as in this picture. It's obviously a lot more difficult to make short hair look longer.

A professional model knows all too well that it's not just her face, but her body as well, that is her fortune, and so she makes a point of keeping in shape. It's all a part of the fantasy of glamour photography.

STRENGTHS AND WEAKNESSES

GLAMOUR BASICS

IT'S THE PICTURES THAT COUNT

To engage the services of a professional model, the photographer invariably turns first to one of the well-known agencies. All top models are registered with an agency which handles their affairs, finds them work and arranges their fees. They can be located through the local phone book.

The agency holds an index card for each of its models, containing a brief description of her – height, statistics, colour of eyes and hair – together with details of the type of work she undertakes – e.g. glamour, topless, nude. From these, and often from past experience of specific girls, the photographer will make a selection for personal interview.

If you are a professional of Jon Gray's standing, the agency will have no objection to their girls attending a private studio for this preliminary chat. An amateur will find things a little more difficult. If he is not known to the agency, he will first have to prove his integrity, perhaps with some examples of his previous work. If the agency agrees to let him interview their girls, he will probably have to do so on their premises the first time, and until he is better known to them.

When girls are interviewed by Jon, it is usually for a particular job and he will have a specific brief in mind. They come to his studio and meet not just the photographer, but maybe also the client for whom he is working as well as the art director who is master-minding the shoot. Each will have his own view on the type of girl required. Often the girls arrive looking far from glamorous, in old clothes, with untidy hair and little or no make-up. It's not how they look at this meeting that counts, but the way they photograph, and that can be seen in the model's book. The 'book' is a portfolio of pictures, collected from previous assignments, that show the photographer her potential and how she works in front of a camera.

To aid in his selection, Jon also makes a couple of quick test shots of each girl attending the interview. In front of a plain background and with standard lighting, he shoots two Polaroids (instant pictures from a special back fitted to his normal camera) of each in a bikini bottom, one close-up and one full-length.

The pictures serve as an up-to-date record of the model's looks and as a reminder of the girl herself later when final discussions on choice are taking place with the client, art director, and anyone else involved in the shoot.

Two Polaroid test shots of the same model, made by the photographer to assess not only the model's potential, but also to check lighting and set. The actual pictures would be cropped much tighter to exclude the unwanted detail seen in the tests.

Two more tests of a different model. The first is a straightforward bikini shot that would have been taken at the time of the girl's initial interview; the second is also a test of the same girl, taken later during an actual shooting session.

Two more test shots, this time of different girls in different locations, used to give the photographer an indication of the way the final pictures will turn out.

GLAMOUR BASICS

IT'S THE PICTURES THAT COUNT

TAKE IT AS RED

Composition plays an important role in all forms of photography. In glamour, it involves two main factors: the model herself – the pose she adopts, the shape of her body within the picture area; and the background or location – how she relates to it and interacts with it. A simple approach to composition is invariably the best.

Little could be simpler than the use, in these shots, of two louvre doors. For maximum impact they have been painted red and contrasted with white, both in the background and in the model's costume. The combination of red and white is one of the most dramatic of all (*Life* magazine used it to effect in their logo for many, many years). Certain colours in the spectrum seem to advance in a picture, while others recede. Red is the colour that advances more than any other, so it is not normally used as a straightforward background: placed behind the model, it would seem to crowd her and dominate the picture too much. Notice, then, that Jon has used the doors here, not as a straight background, but more as props that, both in their position and in their dominance of the picture, are on an equal footing with the model. In one shot, she is even slightly *behind* the doors. Also, their strength has been diluted by the area of white between them, giving a loose impression of a doorway between the two strips of red.

Notice too the way the two doors have been slightly angled. The impression of an opening is therefore heightened, while the horizontal slats turn into small verticals that direct your eye towards the model who is, after all, the principal subject of the picture. The white area behind the model also draws your eye while, by the same token, the dark tone of the doors prevents your eye from wandering out of the picture area, once again concentrating it on the real centre of interest.

In this way, the doors give strength to the shot, while remaining in a subordinate role to the model. As such, the picture is a perfect example of composition.

Red is a strong colour and one that should be used with extreme care in backgrounds. Here it has been diluted both by the strip of white and by the model who is posed within the background, rather than in front of it.

The effect of the doors is enhanced by the model's pose, as if she was standing in a real doorway, while the louvred slats direct the viewer's eye towards the principal subject.

TAKE IT AS RED

DON'T LOSE THE MODEL

Sometimes the background becomes the star of the picture with the model, at first glance, appearing to play the subordinate role. When you come to analyse it however, you'll find that once again the picture relies on an interaction between the two for its effect. Taking a shot like this of a model in front of a tropical waterfall, you can see how each plays its part in the overall success of the picture. The waterfall is naturally vast and so must be shown to be so. Despite that, the model must not be lost in the picture area and so, although she is small in comparison to the background, she is placed in a very strong position compositionally. Pictures divide naturally into thirds and any object placed along one of the thirds always draws the eye. In this picture, the model has been placed along the length of the lower third to make a strong horizontal line which breaks the strength of the heavy vertical lines of falling water. Any form of costume or other major accessories would be totally out of place in a shot like this. The location calls for a completely naked or – as in this case – an all but naked model. Think how out of place a dress or a shirt would be in such a picture and how it would ruin the atmosphere of the shot. And yet see how effective the single flower in her hair is, its small splash of colour drawing the eye to the model and adding just that little extra that turns a good glamour shot into a great one.

Sometimes the background is so spectacular that it could become the star of the picture, but in glamour photography it must always play a subordinate role. This picture is so composed that the waterfall complements the model, and does not detract attention from her.

DON'T LOSE THE MODEL

PUTTING BACKGROUNDS IN THEIR PLACE

Locations can be made to act as a strong element in the picture, as a distinct part of the pose and composition, or as no more than a background to the girl. It depends, among other things, on camera angle and focusing. Here are two shots of the same model in the same location, taken within a few minutes of each other, and yet each shot has a different flavour. In the three-quarter-length shot, the background is a very definite part of the picture. The dense undergrowth seems to surround the girl, giving the impression that she is in the midst of it. That's because it is sharply defined and probably takes up more of the picture area than the model herself. Despite that, the undergrowth is of a fairly uniform colour and texture and, on its own, has no pictorial merit whatsoever. That way it's kept in its place and prevented from dominating the picture. The viewer is left in no doubt about the main point of interest.

In the head and shoulders pose, Jon has moved in closer with two results. The

first is technical. Because depth of field is reduced as the camera-to-subject distance is lessened, the background has been thrown out of focus. The second result is purely pictorial. The undergrowth now no longer seems to surround the model. It has been put in its rightful position in the background, where the fuzzy colour contrasts well with the warmth of the model's skin tones.

Two other points are worth noticing about these pictures. The first is the use of the peacock's feathers to make a simple but effective prop, their colours harmonizing, not only with the background, but also with the model's eyes. The second point is the model herself and the lighting. Jon has chosen a blonde to pose in this location, knowing that a brunette's hair colour would not stand out nearly as clearly against this particular background. Finally, he has photographed the girl against the light, so that the sun shines through her hair, giving it a brilliant halo.

Sometimes the background becomes an integral part of the picture. The camera angle here has given a very real impression that the model is surrounded by jungle.

By contrast to the previous picture, the photographer has moved in close for this shot, using differential focusing techniques to separate the model from the background.

GLAMOUR BASICS

PUTTING BACKGROUNDS IN THEIR PLACE

THE FANTASY FACTOR

The best glamour photography blends model and location together, in a sometimes natural, sometimes surprising combination, while still ensuring that the model herself is the main point of interest. Often a 'found' location can be adapted to the purpose; at other times, a natural location is adapted by the photographer to his own ends. What makes this particular combination of model and location particularly pleasing is the air of normality supplied by the raft in exactly the place you'd expect to see it in one of these regions, but with the unexpected addition of a beautiful naked girl in command. Immediately, an air of fantasy is introduced, a factor which plays a very strong part in the composition of any glamour picture.

A raft in these surroundings is perfectly normal, but the girl gives the picture an air of glamorous fantasy.

THE FANTASY FACTOR

UNUSUAL ACCESSORIES

Often, small details make a big difference to a picture. Here are two shots taken by Jon Gray at the same location with the same model. His personal preference is for the one without the fish. He likes the clean simplicity of the shot, the strong lines of composition in the model's body and the subtle lighting. His client preferred the second shot. Why? Perhaps because it makes the girl look more approachable, more attainable – a strong factor in the appeal of any glamour picture. But the addition of those fish must also account for the extra appeal of this second shot. There is, undeniably, something erotic about the touch of certain objects against bare flesh. The fish, in this picture, perfectly complement the location and the pose while, at the same time, adding that small note of eroticism that makes all the difference to the picture's final appeal.

Which is the better, the photographer's choice of picture or the client's? Of the two pictures shown on these pages, Jon Gray preferred this one for its sheer simplicity.

The fish add an extra
element of eroticism, and
it was this picture that
the client chose for his
calendar.

GLAMOUR BASICS

UNUSUAL ACCESSORIES

SOMETHING SLIGHTLY WICKED

Sometimes it's the incongruous that gives a glamour picture its impact. What makes a pose like this one seem just a little wicked is the accessories and the model's poise. The hairstyle, the necklace and the earrings, the composure of her expression, the single rose, all contribute to making her seem like a certain type of woman. A well-to-do lady in a big country house, caught in the middle of flower arranging, perhaps. In fact, the very last person you'd expect to see wearing a see-through dress as revealing as this one. A topless pose, without the benefit of the accessories would have been far less appealing, and not nearly such a successful glamour picture.

A pose like this is a very obvious and 'traditional' type of glamour picture.

Set against the blatant
sexuality of the image
opposite, a pose like this
one is far more subtle
and, in its own way,
more erotic.

SOMETHING SLIGHTLY WICKED

INTRODUCING THE BIZARRE

While many glamour poses work because they appear natural, others rely on the bizarre for their effect. This picture is one such. Nothing about it, from the costume to the accessories and the lighting is natural, yet the sum total of these factors make an extremely evocative picture. Using the wire netting in front of the model, rather than as a background, immediately gives the picture a 'lady in distress' feeling, emphasized by the dress that appears to be torn and the addition of a gun. But nothing is for real in glamour photography, and so the gun is obviously a toy. A real weapon would have given the picture a far more sinister atmosphere that would have been out of place in this type of photography. A final touch of the unusual is given by the lighting. One flash unit has been placed directly behind the model, so that she blocks it with her body, and fitted with a green gel that gives its effect to her extravagant hairstyle, while contrasting strongly with the red of her dress and colour of the toy gun.

Costume, lighting and
accessories all contribute
to the look of this picture
the bizarre is another
facet of the world of
glamour photography.

INTRODUCING THE BIZARRE

GLAMOUR BASICS

SHOOTING WHEN YOU SHOULDN'T

A naked girl lying on a beach: what could be more representative of the popular view of glamour photography? Yet, even here, in this simple and seemingly ordinary pose, it's the small details that make all the difference to the picture. The framing has been carefully arranged to isolate and concentrate on the upper area of the model's body, ignoring her legs.

The picture was shot at what is usually considered to be entirely the 'wrong' time of day. It is traditionally assumed that you can't take good glamour pictures when the sun is high in the sky; but with the model lying down, rather than sitting or standing, the otherwise unsatisfactory overhead lighting perfectly illuminates her body without the need for reflectors or fill-in flash for any additional effect. In such a pose and at such a time, the girl must keep her eyes shut, otherwise she would be looking directly into the sun. So the closed eyes become a factor controlling the rest of the pose, which in this picture has been arranged to look lazy, almost sleep-like. The position of her arms, carefully placed to appear perfectly casual, gives the impression of total relaxation, while helping, compositionally, to lead your eye along the length of her body. The picture is, in fact, full of horizontal lines – the girl, the sand and the sea beyond – and horizontal lines in any picture give a feeling of rest, which again complements the pose. Finally, there's the addition of the flowers which give the picture a focal point and, in their own way, add a statement about the girl.

When the sun is high in the sky, it is usually considered to be the wrong time of day for successful glamour photography, but when the model lies down, top lighting can be particularly flattering.

SHOOTING WHEN YOU SHOULDN'T

DETAILS THAT MAKE THE DIFFERENCE

The model's pose is at the heart of every successful glamour picture. Put a professional model in front of the camera and she is capable of falling naturally into a number of set poses that she knows look good on film, and many of which can be used as a basis for what the photographer is out to achieve. A less experienced girl needs a lot more direction.

The worst thing the photographer can do is stand his model in front of a background, bury his head in the viewfinder and wait for her to do something. Getting the pose right calls for a close working relationship between the photographer and model, each of whom should try to understand not only the other's requirements, but also his or her

difficulties and problems.

The first pose assumed by the model is rarely the best one. Having directed her into it, the photographer must keep shooting and making minor adjustments until everything looks exactly right. Sometimes the smallest movement of the body, a hand or a leg, can make a big difference to the overall effect.

Always remember that the model is a living, breathing human being, not just another prop to be moved around in the studio. Talk to her while you are posing her, tell her what you are trying to achieve, encourage her, tell her when something looks good. Tell her it's good even when it isn't, then make the adjustment to make it better. Get her

involved, show her your enthusiasm and you'll get hers in return.

Working in a studio, a little background music can make all the difference in helping to relax both the model and photographer. It sounds an obvious thing, but don't forget that she is undressed and probably colder than you are. Make sure she's warm enough. Keep her comfortable in a pose: you'll never get good pictures from a cold or uncomfortable model.

There are a lot of so-called rules about posing, but really they all come down to one, basic factor: does it look good? If the pose looks right, shoot it. Then improve on it and shoot again. Don't start on a new pose until you have thoroughly exhausted all the possibilities of the first.

Sometimes the smallest movement of a hand or leg can make all the difference to a pose. A picture like this one would be just one of many variations.

Sometimes the most
incongruous poses make
the best pictures. The
bottom line when it
comes to posing is
simply: if it looks good,
shoot it.

GLAMOUR BASICS

DETAILS THAT MAKE THE DIFFERENCE

DOING WHAT COMES NATURALLY

Perhaps *the* most important aspect of any glamour pose is its naturalness. However a girl is posed, whatever the location, irrespective of the overall mood of the picture, she must look natural. The slightest sign of self-consciousness will detract from the success of the picture.

Strange as it may seem, naturalness does not come naturally. Looking relaxed and natural in what is often the most unnatural of surroundings is an art all its own. The way the model holds herself, the position of her arms and legs, her expression, all play their part in making the pose look completely natural. For the inexperienced or amateur model it can be one of the most difficult aspects of the job.

In such circumstances, it is up to the photographer to relax his model. He does that by clear instructions, using little trade secrets that he knows will have the desired effect and by showing confidence in everything she does, encouraging her, never criticizing her and generally helping her through the session.

If a girl really wants to model, she will soon unwind and, although she might feel tense and awkward at the beginning, with help and guidance from the photographer she will soon gain confidence, relax and begin giving her best.

Naturalness is one of the most important facets of glamour photography. Whatever the pose or location, it's important that the model looks and feels at ease in what she is doing.

Sometimes the credibility
of a model's naturalness
can be stretched. But
providing she can look at
home in even the most
unusual locations, the
picture will be a winner.

DOING WHAT COMES NATURALLY

GLAMOUR BASICS

A STANDING START

Legs make a good starting point for any pose. The way they are positioned can make a big difference to the rest of the model's body. If your model is standing, it is rarely advisable to shoot her head-on. It is better to turn her so that her legs are seen in three-quarters or profile view. Don't let her keep them both straight. A small change in position here can make all the difference to implied movement in a pose, changing it from something static to something more dynamic.

Don't feel that you must always show the whole of your subject's legs. Many good glamour poses are cut off at the knee or above, accentuating the rest of the body. If you *are* going to shoot her legs in full, do so with a pose that makes them

the real centre of interest. Alternatively, photograph her sitting or kneeling, but take care with the latter that the lower part of her leg is not hidden by the rest making it appear that you have truncated your model at the knee.

Lighting is important when legs are featured prominently. It is all too easy to light your subject for her face and the main part of her body, allowing it to fall off below the knee. The result is under-exposure and what can easily look like dirty legs. Once the lighting has been set up, then, exposure readings should be taken from your model's face, all the way down to her feet. If the reading is lower at any point, the lighting must be readjusted to equalize its effect all over.

Take care not to let your model's calves, ankles or thighs look too thick. A wrong camera angle can turn the most beautiful of legs into monsters; a slight change of camera angle often corrects the fault.

When it comes to feet, try not to let your model stand flat-footed. Feet are ugly things at the best of times and the camera can very easily make them look even uglier. Ask her to point her toes or stand on tip-toe as you take the picture. High-heeled shoes will do the job for you, while adding to the picture a traditionally erotic element all their own. Watch out, too, for toe-nails: if they are to be seen in the picture, the model should take as much care of them as she does her finger-nails.

Legs are usually best shot in profile and with the model's weight falling more on one than the other.

In a sitting pose, the
model's legs can be
accentuated to become
the focal point of the
picture.

A STANDING START

GLAMOUR BASICS

BODY BEAUTIFUL

The breasts and stomach are very often the focal point of a glamour picture and must be posed to look their most attractive.

The way a girl holds her body will have different effects on her breasts. Leaning forward into a pose with her arms close to her sides will help to make small breasts look larger. Leaning back will separate them and make them look smaller. Shape and form will be accentuated in a girl with an average-sized bust when she pulls back her shoulders. A larger-than-average bust will look more attractive if you ask the model to stretch her arms above her head, tensing her muscles and so lifting her breasts slightly.

A topless shot works best if the model is not absolutely head-on to the camera. Turned slightly aside or in a three-quarters view, she will usually look more attractive, but care must be taken with camera angles to ensure that one breast doesn't look larger than the other.

Stomachs are attractive only when they are flat. A professional model who looks after her body will usually have a naturally flat stomach, but slight bulges can be taken care of by asking her to breathe in at the moment of exposure. Make sure, however, that doing so does not affect her expression. Asking a model to take a deep breath and then to hold it while you take a few exposures can easily result in an unnatural, strained expression.

Watch, too, for creases in your model's skin as she turns into a pose. Twisting her body one way or the other can easily lead to lines appearing around her waist. Asking her to stretch slightly in a direction away from the creases can often iron them out and so make a far more attractive pose.

All these points are for the photographer to watch. The model will only react to what you tell her to do and won't necessarily be aware of problems like lines and creases that the pose is creating. So keep a careful eye on them and, where necessary, take action to eliminate them.

Stomachs are really attractive only when they are flat. Slight bulges can be taken care of by asking the model to breathe in at the moment of exposure.

Topless shots look best when the model is not facing squarely towards the camera. A three-quarters view is far more attractive.

BODY BEAUTIFUL

ARMS AND HANDS

Arms and hands can often cause the worst problems in poses. It is all too easy for your model to look very self-conscious about the way they are placed.

It's best, therefore, to give the hands something to do and the arms will then follow naturally. This can mean asking your model to place her hands confidently on some part of her own body: a hand on a thigh; on her shoulders, arms across her breasts; one arm across her body, fingers resting lightly on the other arm; flicking fingers through her hair. Or you can add props, something for the hands to hold: a mirror and comb, a flower, a sea-shell if you are on the beach. Again, hands and arms can be used in conjunction with some larger prop: resting naturally against a tree, reaching up for its fruit, spread out along the back of a seat.

Camera angles must be watched very carefully in relation to arms and hands. If one is nearer to the camera than the other, it might look very much larger. Shoulders, too, can look out of proportion if one is too near the camera. The effect is worsened by short focal length lenses, but conversely can be cured by the use of longer focal lengths, or just a small change in camera angle.

Care must also be taken not to chop off hands unnecessarily. A pose that involves an arm truncated at the wrist can look weird and ugly.

If hands are to feature prominently in the picture, finger-nails are important. Your model's should be well-shaped and, if desired, painted with a colour that matches her costume and lipstick.

In a sitting pose, arms and hands fall naturally along the legs, giving a relaxed look to the picture.

Giving the model something to hold is one way to deal with the problem of hands. The use of the mirror in this picture makes the position of both the girl's arms and hands appear perfectly natural.

ARMS AND HANDS

SMILE PLEASE

A nice relaxed smile works wonders for a glamour pose, but learning to smile naturally is not as easy as it sounds. A natural smile involves more than a curl of the lips – it puts light into the eyes too. Ask an amateur model to smile and, very often, she will react with her mouth, while her eyes remain dead. The result is a forced expression. Ask a professional model to smile and, very often, she will start by looking away from the camera completely, and then turn back smiling as she does so. You can use the same trick to produce a natural expression in a less experienced model. The movement will take her mind off the actual act of smiling and the result will be a lot more natural on film.

A model new to glamour work is often nervous. Remember that and do all you can to help her relax. Nerves build up tension in facial muscles and so lead to unnatural expressions. Asking her to fill her mouth with air and puff it out a few times will help her to relax this area – and because it's also a pretty silly exercise, it often leads to laughter and a far more natural, relaxed expression.

Smiling, pouting or just looking serious . . . they are all expressions that the trained model has learnt to adopt to perfection.

SMILE PLEASE

GLAMOUR BASICS

MAKE-UP FOR THE CAMERA

Make-up for glamour photography is basically an exaggerated version of a girl's normal way of preparing her face. It is used for several reasons. The first and foremost is obviously to make the model look more glamorous. But make-up is used for other, more technical reasons too. One is to prevent shine and unwanted highlights from the studio lighting on the surface of her skin. Another is to define her features better in long shots. A professional glamour photographer like Jon Gray works primarily for publication, and printing processes are notorious for destroying fine detail. So when shooting a three-quarter- or full-length picture, make-up is best overdone a little. Moving in closer, more care must be taken and the make-up made gentler, less dramatic. It's all too easy for make-up effects to be over- or underdone and the view you see with the naked eye is rarely matched by the result on film. A test shot on instant film, with the model posed under the chosen lighting set-up, will tell the photographer if he is actually getting the effect he is after.

Most professional models know exactly the type of make-up that suits their particular face and can apply it themselves. It is quite common, however, for the photographer to employ an independent make-up artist to prepare the model in exactly the way needed for a specific picture. Unless a deliberately off-beat effect, demanding the use of specialist make-up, is being sought, most of the products needed can be found in a normal cosmetic store. Theatrical suppliers can add anything that is a little more out of the ordinary.

Make-up is chosen to match the pose, in this case little more than an exaggerated version of what the girl might wear for an ordinary night out.

Occasionally, make-up is used to more dramatic effect. In cases like this, the photographer will often employ a professional make-up artist to prepare the model's face.

MAKE-UP FOR THE CAMERA

GLAMOUR BASICS

FACING UP TO MAKE-UP

Here are the main stages in make-up for a fairly conventional glamour picture. The first is the application of foundation. This has a slight tint and is used to disguise any slight blemishes in the model's skin. Powder is used next. It's translucent and used to prevent shine from the lights and as an aid to ensure that make-up lasts longer. The powder is pressed gently in, then the excess is dusted off. Blusher is applied slightly under the cheek-bone to help give the face shape, but care must be taken not to overdo the colour (this is a good place to check the effect with a Polaroid). Highlighter is used above the cheek-bone and blended with the blusher to give a gradual change from one to the other. No hard lines should be seen between the two. Eye-shadow is applied thickly, then gently smudged to blend softly with the areas around the eyes; then mascara is added to accentuate the eyelashes. Lips come last, with a colour chosen to complement the pose, matched with accessories and nail varnish. The lips are first outlined with a fine brush in a colour a shade darker than the chosen one. This way, thin lips can be made to look fuller, large lips can be slimmed down and lips that are slightly crooked can be straightened. Lipstick and gloss in the chosen colour are then added, usually with a small brush, inside the already drawn line.

Correctly applied make-up is particularly important when the photographer is moving in for tight close-ups like this.

A good translucent powder is used to prevent any suggestion of shine from the studio lights.

For a rather more exotic
type of picture, the
model's make-up can be
slightly exaggerated.

FACING UP TO MAKE-UP

PUTTING ON THE STYLE

The style, the shape and the cut of a model's hair can make all the difference to the pose and the final effect of the picture. As with so much in this type of photography, simplicity is the best approach and few models have elaborate or individual hairstyles. Instead, they have it cut simply, keep it in a healthy condition, and usually wear it at around shoulder length. On that basis, they can build different styles to suit the required pose. Long hair can be worn up to appear shorter; it can be curled, either lightly or tightly, with a simple set of heated rollers; it can be slicked back with water or a gel.

Called to a session, the model will usually arrive with her hair freshly washed and, if she colours it, recently tinted to prevent dark roots. If necessary, she will put it in rollers while she is preparing her make-up.

Worn up, her hair will give her face a fairly cool, sophisticated look; with her hair down, she will look sexier. Perhaps for that reason, pictures of long-haired girls usually sell better than those with short hair. It's just another consideration the professional glamour photographer must take into account when he chooses a model.

A model will rarely have an elaborate hairstyle of her own. Instead, she will have a simple cut that she knows can be used in different ways: down around her shoulders, high on her head or even wet. Each adds its own touch to the final effect of the pose.

PUTTING ON THE STYLE

ONE STEP FURTHER

So far, we've looked at the fundamental make-up of glamour photography, Jon Gray style. We've looked at what makes a good model, how to find the girls that most suit different types of picture and the basics of posing. Now we're going to go further and look at all those special details that make the difference between a mediocre glamour picture and a good glamour picture. Then we're going further still – into the extra considerations that turn good pictures into great ones. Jon Gray is a successful glamour photographer. Read on and you'll learn about the techniques that have taken him to the top.

Sometimes the surroundings are as important as the model. The large mirror and the ornate bedroom used for this picture are every bit as vital as the model's pose.

A strong, rather blatant pose that is enhanced by the starkness of the set, the harshness of the lighting and the model's direct, challenging expression.

Two girls, simple poses and props, plus a restricted use of colour have all added their mood to the overall effect of this shot.

ONE STEP FURTHER

SUCCESSFUL GLAMOUR PHOTOGRAPHY

ONE STEP FURTHER

Warm evening light and a lush location each add to the element of fantasy, so important in top-class glamour photography.

Two pictures that use settings in different ways. In the exterior shot, the background is simple, but still interesting. In the studio picture, the setting dominates the model and has become an integral part of the pose itself.

Two different types of studio shot, each blending model and background in a different way. In one, a location has been suggested by the use of foliage and dry ice. In the other, the background is far more abstract, complementing the model's pose and costume.

Natural props, found on
location, can often help
the pose.

SUCCESSFUL GLAMOUR PHOTOGRAPHY

ONE STEP FURTHER

STARTING SIMPLY

Glamour photography is very much a contradiction of its own terms. Its effect is reliant on the charms of a naked model, yet nudity in itself is seldom enough to create the atmosphere that good glamour photography always generates. Rather, it is the interaction of the model, what little clothing she does wear and the setting.

In this picture of a model against a white pillar, that combination has been reduced to ultimate simplicity. The pillar itself influences the whole picture, its thin, straight line echoed by the model's body. Normal clothing in a pose like this would seem completely out of place, whereas the somewhat incongruous addition of shoes and hat has added a slightly surreal feeling to the mood of the shot. Her averted gaze adds another touch to that mood. The background, produced by out-of-focus patches of paint on ordinary background paper, blends perfectly with the cool white of the pillar and contrasts with the model's skin tones, so accentuating her presence. The final result is a subtle blend of form and shape, girl and props, to produce an unusual, even disturbing image.

A simple setting can be very effective. The white pillar, the pose and what little clothing the model wears – each contributes to a successful image.

CHANGING FANTASY INTO REALITY

In complete contrast to the previous picture of the girl against a white pillar, this shot of a girl in red boxing gloves is very hard, very 'real'. Once again the element of fantasy plays its part – whoever saw a boxer like this? – but the interaction of the model, the props and the setting has made the fantasy seem real. The hardness of the lighting, the direct look of the model, the dramatic use of red and the tile-like background that suggests changing-rooms and showers all add to the reality, while the very fact that an attractive and rather vulnerable-looking girl has been depicted in what is essentially a tough man's world, introduces the note of fantasy. Taken to extremes, some glamour poses and set-ups can verge on the ridiculous. The art of the professional glamour photographer is never to let things get that far.

Fantasy plays a strong part in most glamour photography. What makes this picture work is the presence of the girl in what is obviously a man's domain.

More fantasy with an attractive girl in a man's world. In situations like this, the photographer must guard against allowing the pose to go too far, keeping it just on this side of reality.

CHANGING FANTASY INTO REALITY

SUCCESSFUL GLAMOUR PHOTOGRAPHY

BRINGING THE BACKGROUND FORWARD

The model and her setting should always complement one another. This can be done by using contrasts, or it can be more sympathetic – as in the picture shown here of a girl and an old camera. The first unusual aspect of this setting is the camera itself, and that largely controls everything else. Its richly polished mahogany and brass provide warm, almost sepia colours, around which the set has been built. The colour of the model's hair matches the colours of the camera, and her skin tones have been warmed by the use of an 81B filter. Added to that, a sheet of ordinary background paper, also chosen for its warm hue, has been positioned in front of the model, rather than in its usual place behind her, and then cut and rolled away, making a suitable gap through which she is seen, posed against a second, this time black, length of paper. Her eyes are averted from the camera and she seems to be wrapped up in her own thoughts. The pose, together with the spy-hole effect produced by the cut paper in the foreground, give the impression that she is unaware of the photographer's presence, thus giving the shot a slightly voyeuristic appeal that, when executed with taste, is yet another aspect of glamour photography.

The 'background' doesn't always have to be behind the model. In this case, a roll of background paper has been cut and placed in front of her.

How props and pose can blend together. The rich colours of the old camera make a perfect foil for the warmth of the model's hair and skin tones.

BRINGING THE BACKGROUND FORWARD

ONE GIRL, TWO MOODS

Background and props play a part in glamour photography but, at the end of the day, they are there only as accessories to the model and her pose. Take them away and you are down to basics: one girl, the simplest of backgrounds . . . and the photographer's imagination. Here are two ways that Jon Gray has handled that situation, using the same model, without the benefit of any accessory except a plain background, to produce pictures with two very distinct moods.

The background in both pictures is perfectly plain, supplied by a length of seamless paper. In one shot, the colour has been chosen deliberately to contrast with the model's skin tones, the lighting is hard and the model looks directly and unashamedly at the camera. Everything about her pose is direct and challenging. The second picture couldn't be more different. Again, a backdrop of seamless paper has been used, but this time in a colour which harmonizes with the model's skin tones. The effect is warm, rather than the cold look of the previous picture. By seating the model and posing her this way, her body has become a compact collection of smoothly-flowing curves, almost an abstract pattern; she is no longer the overt sex object portrayed in the first picture. By facing her slightly away and at an angle, the viewer is given the impression of a private moment, as though the girl is wrapped in her own thoughts, almost unaware of the camera.

One girl, two pictures, two very different moods. Producing these is all part of the glamour photographer's art.

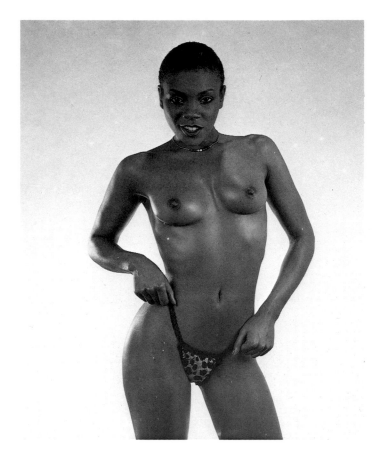

Backgrounds can make all the difference to a picture's mood. Here the colour contrasts with the model's skin tones, reinforcing the hardness of the pose.

In contrast to the previous shot, this background has been chosen to blend with the model, to give a softer, gentler effect.

ONE GIRL, TWO MOODS

SUCCESSFUL GLAMOUR PHOTOGRAPHY

SOFT FOCUS

In the picture of the Japanese girl, once again simplicity is the keynote. She has no costume and no props. The picture works through no more than her pose and the simplest of backgrounds: white, seamless paper and the addition of a couple of palm fronds which so complement the model. But here, the photographer has added one very subtle extra in the form of a little soft focus to the image.

Soft focus is not *lack* of focus. The picture is sharp enough, but the image is softened so that highlights spread slightly into shadow areas. It works best when the softening is at the edges, leaving the centre of the picture area clearly defined in the normal way. There are a number of ways of achieving this effect, from ultra-expensive soft-focus lenses to inexpensive filters. Most photographers, however, prefer to make their own devices. All that's needed is a way to break up the image, to scatter light rays as they travel through the lens to the film. Jon Gray uses two of the more popular methods. One is to take a clear filter such as a UV, or a piece of flat glass, and smear just a little petroleum jelly (the trade name in the UK is Vaseline) lightly around the edges, leaving the central area clear, and then to shoot through that. His second method is to stretch pieces of clear adhesive tape across the edges of a lens hood, again leaving the centre clear, then to shoot with that in position on the lens. In both cases, the effect varies with the lens aperture in use: the wider the aperture, the better the effect. Once more, Jon has proved that you don't need sophisticated props or complicated sets to take good glamour pictures.

There are many soft-focus devices on the market, but one of the most effective is also one of the least expensive: simply, a little petroleum jelly smeared around the edges of a clear filter.

SOFT FOCUS

WATER MAGIC

What could be a more natural subject for a glamour pose than a beautiful girl taking a shower? As in the pictures on the previous few pages, Jon has taken the concept and reduced it to the barest simplicity, knowing that, handled in the right way, the combination of nudity and water will work its usual magic. Needless to say, the picture wasn't produced in a real shower, but in the studio. A dark background has been chosen to ensure that the water droplets will stand out and the use of strong side lighting has given the water an extra sparkle – the speed of the studio flash catching every drop as it falls or bounces from the model's body. The shower itself was supplied by an assistant up a ladder with a watering-can and, just for the record, the picture was taken on a very cold day. Sometimes it's necessary for the model to suffer a little for the sake of the final effect.

Seemingly natural surroundings can make top glamour pictures – even when the reality is far from natural. In this case, the 'shower' was provided by a watering-can held by the photographer's assistant up a ladder.

WATER MAGIC

THE GOOD, THE BAD AND THE RIDICULOUS

Who can define eroticism? It's all things to all people. Rarely is it present just in a model's pose; rather, it is a combination of pose, setting and costume. Especially the costume. Because however eroticism is defined, one fact holds true: a partially clothed body is always more erotic than a totally naked one. Part of the appeal lies not in what the viewer can actually see, but in what the picture suggests he *shouldn't* be seeing. So see-through garments, dresses with plunging necklines, slit skirts, all play their part. Certain fabrics, like satin and lace, give this desired effect, as do certain colours – black, white, red – and certain items of underwear: why else would so many glamour poses involve the incongruous combination of stockings, suspenders and high-heeled shoes, and little else besides?

The dividing line between what is erotic and what is tasteless or, for that matter, downright laughable, is a fine one. The glamour photographer seeking to portray eroticism (and not all glamour photography necessarily has to be erotic), must tread a careful path, balancing cheekiness with a sexual image while keeping a wary eye on the twin perils of bad taste and the ridiculous. When the photographer gets it right, the result is a picture that can be appreciated as much by women as by men; when he gets it wrong, he should be able to judge his work objectively and to destroy the pictures. There is little worse in photography than bad glamour.

A partially clothed body is always more erotic than one that is totally nude.

Certain items of clothing such as high heels or, as in this case, a see-through skirt, always enhance the eroticism of a picture.

SUCCESSFUL GLAMOUR PHOTOGRAPHY

THE GOOD, THE BAD AND THE RIDICULOUS

KEEP IT TASTEFUL

Second to costume, background and props can add their own touches to the eroticism of a picture. Take a picture of a partially clothed girl in a studio setting and, although glamorous, it might not be erotic. Put her in the same pose in a more ordinary setting – a kitchen or an office maybe – and the juxtaposition of nudity with unexpected but familiar surroundings introduces a new note of eroticism. Similarly with props: a fireman's hose with its phallic undertones; guns, providing they are obviously not real ones; some of the milder fetishes. Used with good taste and a little humour, they all contribute to the erotic element of a glamour picture. But the photographer must take care over staying on the right side of what is tasteful. There is no room for bad taste or pornography in genuine glamour photography.

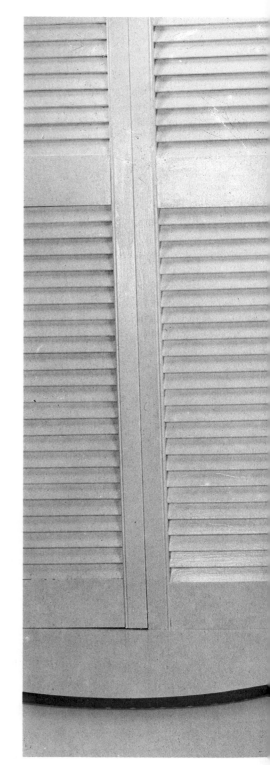

Certain props will add to the erotic element of a picture, but the photographer must always stay on the right side of good taste.

KEEP IT TASTEFUL

TAKE TWO GIRLS

Much of Jon Gray's work involves location shooting with two or three models, and occasionally girls are used in pairs or even in threes in one picture. Such pictures have to be very carefully arranged. The moment two or more girls appear together, nuances are created that must be controlled. Some glamour photographers make a point of shooting with two girls, producing pictures which, while tasteful, have very definite suggestions of lesbianism. Such pictures are not Jon Gray's style. When two or more girls appear in his pictures, they are shown to be aware of one another's presence, but in no way sexually involved with each other. They rarely touch, except in ways that are totally innocent or in others where perhaps the final effect is slightly surreal.

Such self-imposed restrictions make posing difficult. When two or more girls appear in Jon's pictures, it is in circumstances in which girls might *normally* be half-dressed and together: in a changing-room, swimming, sun bathing on the beach. Rarely do they look at each other. Eye contact again introduces too much familiarity to the picture.

Alternatively, they might be used together merely as a combination of shapes, perhaps one lying, one standing, one sitting; the combination of their poses making an abstract pattern against the background.

To pose two or three models in the same picture, while still retaining an element of glamour in its truest sense, is a job for the professional and should not be undertaken lightly by the amateur photographer unless he is very sure of both himself and his models.

Poses with two girls work best in locations where nudity is natural. The beach and sea are perfect examples.

When two girls are posed together, they should be seen to be aware of one another's presence, but in no way sexually involved.

TAKE TWO GIRLS

A TOUCH OF THE UNUSUAL

Some of the most ordinary, everyday objects can be used as effective props in glamour photography. In these two pictures, Jon Gray has used toy balloons, gas filled to make them lighter than air. The shape and texture of balloons make a perfect foil for a model's figure and, in this case, their unusual colour works well against both her skin tones and the dramatic blackness of the background.

In the first shot, the balloons act as an accessory, matching the colour of the model's boots, adding composition to the abstract shape of the pose and offering just that little touch of the unusual that makes a good glamour photograph so attractive. The actual pose would have worked quite well without the balloons, but is improved by their addition. In the second shot, the balloons are the whole point of the picture. Without them, it would have had little attraction – just another half-naked girl facing the camera. They add mystery, humour and – to those who look for such things – they symbolize the anonymity of the glamour model, known for her body, not for her face.

Both of these pictures are very professional in their execution, yet they use a setting and props that could have been utilized by even the most inexperienced amateur photographer.

Simple accessories, but they add a lot to a picture. Here, the colour, shape and the texture of the balloons contribute to the mood of the picture.

In contrast to the picture opposite, the balloons have been used here not as an addition to the pose, but as an essential ingredient to the style and meaning of the shot.

A TOUCH OF THE UNUSUAL

USING DRY ICE

The most exotic effects are often created by the simplest of means. A steamy atmosphere can lend a note of eroticism to a shot and is easily produced by the use of dry ice.

Dry ice is the common name for frozen carbon dioxide. It is readily obtainable from theatrical furnishers: check your local phone book for the nearest. The substance is super-cold and will burn if it comes into contact with the skin. Use it only with rubber gloves – and keep it well away from your model!

Dropped into a bucket of water, the substance produces a dense, white steam. It works with cold water, but the warmer the water, the better the effect. Unlike real steam, this is cool and is heavier than air. It hugs the ground and builds up layer by layer, so is useful for simulating rising mist from a swampy jungle, for instance. The steam itself is harmless to the skin and it can be blown around your model, either with a professional wind-machine – a large, heavy-duty fan – or simply by fanning it with a piece of cardboard. Once in the water, dry ice soon melts, so buy more than you think you need and work quickly.

Although the steam is harmless to the touch, it must not be inhaled, so use it only at ground level and don't ask your model to lie in it or take up any pose that involves her head being below the 'surface'.

A little dry ice dropped into a bucket of water out of sight of the camera, and fanned on to the set by an assistant, can work wonders in this type of picture.

Dry ice is heavier than air and so builds up from floor level. It can be lit by studio lights to enhance its effect.

USING DRY ICE

WORKING UP A SWEAT

Studio sets made to resemble tropical locations, or others that suggest a lot of exercise, are enhanced if your model's body gleams with a simulated sweat.

The effect is produced not by working her until she really begins to sweat, but by the application of baby oil. The glamour photographer always has a large bottle on hand for the purpose. Ask your model to pour it on and rub it in generously, but make sure that she does so evenly and without streaks, especially around items of clothing. The camera is notorious for picking up every streak if the oil is not applied correctly.

With the right amount, your model's body will shine and gleam in the studio lights, adding a sultry eroticism to the final picture.

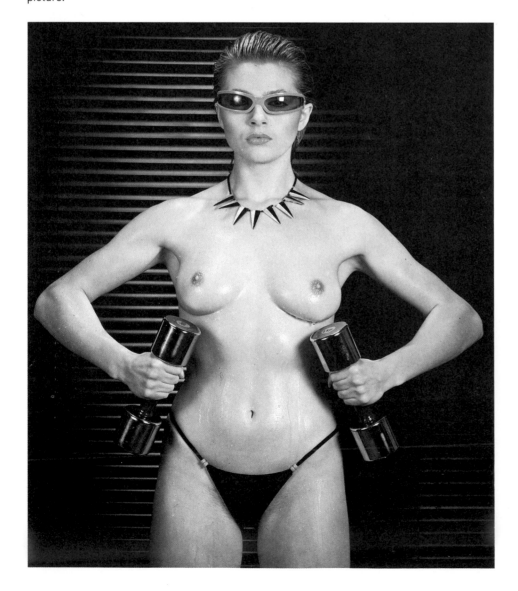

If the pose calls for it, the application of baby oil will make the model's body gleam.

WORKING UP A SWEAT

SNAKES ALIVE!

Some props really are available only to the professional photographer – and to the professional model who takes certain unusual situations in her stride. Make no mistake about it, snakes are for professionals. This one is a very real, live python and, handled the right way, it makes an extremely exotic prop for one of the more unusual types of glamour picture. A snake like this can be dangerous but, providing it is well fed before the session and then kept cool – when they warm up they start to get a bit lively! – it can usually be relied upon to stay where it is put in the set.

Given a prop such as this, it would be all too easy for the photographer to use it and nothing else. But this shot, like so much of Jon Gray's work, is made so much the better by the set, built by simply tying lengths of bamboo together, the model's wild-girl hairstyle and her unusual costume. Together, all those things give the picture its element of eroticism. Danger, in itself, can be erotic when treated the right way, and the portrayal of a beautiful, vulnerable girl in a seemingly dangerous situation adds as much, if not more, to the power of this picture as do her obvious physical charms.

The snake by itself makes an interesting prop, but here it has been enhanced by the set, the model's costume and her wild hairstyle.

SNAKES ALIVE!

THE RULES OF COMPOSITION

Composition, the way various elements are arranged in a picture, is a subtle thing. When it's done well, the viewer doesn't even notice it. He knows only that he sees a pleasing picture. When it's done badly, the viewer will be displeased, but won't necessarily know why. It is up to the photographer, then, to know the rules of composition and to present his pictures in ways that stay within those rules, thus producing the best images.

Some rules of composition apply specifically to glamour photography and not to other kinds. In landscape photography, for instance, the principal subject will usually be depicted off-centre, in juxtaposition with other, less important

subjects. In glamour, the principal subject is the model and, much of the time, she will be depicted full-centre in the picture area. Other rules hold true as much for glamour photography as for any other kind. For example, lines in a picture formed by the girl's body, props or background, give the shot different moods according to their direction. Horizontal lines are restful, vertical lines are more dynamic, diagonal lines imply movement. In its simplest terms, that means that a picture of a girl lying down, or one which contains a lot of horizontal lines – a beach, the sea, the sky beyond – will always have a more relaxed appearance than one in which the model is standing, surrounded perhaps by

trees; while a picture that has a lot of lines diagonally across the frame will give a strong impression of motion.

For the glamour photographer working on a major project like a calendar, picture composition takes on another dimension as well. Having decided on a basic pose and the way in which the girl is to be used with the background, he must shoot as many variations on that pose as he can find. Film is treated for what it is: the cheapest commodity on the trip, and a lot is used to explore different ideas and variations so that, back home, the client has as wide a choice as possible from which to select the pictures that will finally appear on the calendar.

A picture with strong horizontal lines will always look more relaxed than one with a lot of vertical lines.

The glamour photographer, working on a commission, will shoot a number of variations on the same pose from which his client can make the final choice.

Unlike some other forms of photography, glamour often requires the principal subject to be central in the frame.

THE RULES OF COMPOSITION

CROPPING FOR EFFECT

Sometimes the slightest variation can make all the difference to a picture. One interesting point that Jon has found is the way women's reactions to a picture vary, depending on how identifiable the model is. A woman who claims not to like a picture that shows the model's face, will change her mind when she sees a similar picture in which the model's features are hidden, either by pose or, as in this case, by cropping the image in the viewfinder. Shooting a picture like this, Jon has given his client several different aspects of what is, in essence, one idea. He has offered three variations, not only just on the amount of the girl's face that is visible, but also on actual areas of her body. He has also experimented slightly with exposure. As it is increased, so the skin tones have become lighter, also adding variety to the same theme. Another variation he has offered the client is the use of the necklace.

Three variations on a single theme, but notice how the photographer has created a slightly different mood by the use of picture cropping, simple accessories and even adjusting the exposure.

CROPPING FOR EFFECT

PICTURE SHAPES

If you were to draw an imaginary line between certain key areas in a picture, and then analyse the patterns that those lines make, you would find that certain shapes make more pleasing pictures than others. Shapes that have an odd number of corners always seem to work better than those with an even number, and three works best of all. So the triangle is one of the most important shapes in picture composition. Notice how Jon has used that fact in these two pictures.

In the picture of the girl sitting on the tree, there is a very definite triangular shape drawn from her head, down her body to the trunk, along the trunk and then back to her face. Lines that are as strong as those produced by this tree naturally lead the eye from the edge of the picture into its main point of interest. In this picture the viewer's eye is drawn by the implied movement of this diagonal line into the picture and then arrested at the strong vertical lines of the model, focusing on the main centre of interest.

The triangular lines of composition have also been used in the second picture, but this time the shape is formed almost entirely by her body, from her head, down her arms to the trunk, along the trunk to her legs and back. Once again, the shape has had a strong effect on the picture's appeal.

The lines of the tree trunk lead the eye **naturally towards the girl.**

The model's pose in this shot creates a triangular shape, traditional in picture composition.

PICTURE SHAPES

A SENSE OF DIRECTION

A model's position in the picture and the direction in which she is looking are factors which, combined, affect the picture's composition and mood. In general, if the model is on the left of the picture, shot in any stance other than full frontal to the camera, then she should be looking towards the right. If she is on the right, she should look left. The direction in which she looks implies movement, and there should always be space in the picture to 'move into'. As an example, consider the picture of the girl fishing. She is looking towards the right and there is plenty of space on the right for her to look into. Had she been on the right of the picture and still looking in the same direction, the balance would have been destroyed.

When the subject is in the centre of the frame, the direction in which she is looking plays a different part. Often, she will look straight at the camera, giving eye contact with the viewer and consequently a strong appeal. If she looks slightly away, she might appear more pensive. A look right out of the picture's frame will give the impression that she is watching something that the viewer can't see. That's the case in this picture of the girl with the washing basket, and the fact that she *isn't* looking at the camera is part of its appeal: as though she has been caught off-guard and is unaware of being photographed. Little things like that help give the picture its mood.

If movement is implied – in this case towards the direction in which the model is looking – then the picture should have room for the model to 'move into'.

With the model central in the frame, the direction in which she looks can change the mood of the picture. Looking away from the camera as she is here, creates the impression that an unguarded, candid moment has been caught by the photographer.

A SENSE OF DIRECTION

SUCCESSFUL GLAMOUR PHOTOGRAPHY

MAKING LIGHT WORK

Time of day plays its part in picture composition, as weather and light change to give different effects. Here are two pictures, taken in very similar locations. The one shot in bright sunlight is a traditional glamour picture, using a naked girl in the natural environment of the sea and adding the palm branch as a prop to give an extra point of interest, while aiding the composition of an otherwise quite ordinary picture: remember the point about shapes and triangles? The second picture was taken at a very different time of day, one not normally associated with glamour photography at all, but it too has a charm of its own, using the sombre, monochromatic sea and sky, and shooting the model in silhouette for dramatic effect.

Bright sun, sand and sea
. . . all the traditional
components of glamour
photography.

The atmospheric lighting
at the end of a day gives
a different look to what
would otherwise have
been a fairly standard
picture.

AMATEUR LIGHTING, PROFESSIONAL RESULTS

Think of a glamour studio and you instinctively think of expensive, professional set-ups. But a small studio can easily be improvised at home with the minimum of expense.

An ordinary flashgun, fitted to a lighting stand or tripod, bounced into a white umbrella and connected to the camera with a synch lead will give you all the lighting you need to start. The rest can be improvised.

Placing your model in front of a large window and lighting her with the bounced flash just beside the camera gives pleasing results in straightforward head-and-shoulders poses. The flash lights the face, and light from the window gives soft highlights around the hair. The effect works best if the light outside is slightly brighter than that given by the flash – about one stop difference works well.

Reflectors can be used to bounce some light from the window back into the model's face if her eyes are falling into dark pools of shadow or if her hairline is producing another ugly shadow on her forehead. Working at home, reflectors can be improvised with white sheets, tablecloths, or – particularly useful – pieces of white polystyrene usually used for decorating.

If you are posing your model this way in front of a window, watch out for flare caused by direct light from outside falling across your camera lens. A good deep lens hood, or a piece of black cardboard held above the lens, will kill this and give your pictures a much sharper appearance.

A picture like this could be taken as easily in an average-sized living room as in a studio.

Posing the model in front of a window can provide a different background – and one that can be found in most homes.

Simple, plain backgrounds can be made in the home by use of seamless paper, hung from a convenient support.

AMATEUR LIGHTING, PROFESSIONAL RESULTS

SUCCESSFUL GLAMOUR PHOTOGRAPHY

A SIMPLE BACKGROUND

A professional background can be created in the home by using coloured background paper, available in rolls from photographic suppliers. Professionals use the paper in 9-ft widths, but the amateur can buy rolls half that width or buy a professional roll with a friend and cut it in half.

The paper can be suspended from hooks in the wall, or from a specially-made trough on a stand that holds the roll high above the model and allows you to pull it down to floor length. More ambitious is a frame, made for the job, with expandable legs that can be braced between floor and ceiling with the background roll suspended between them.

If you are shooting head and shoulders or three-quarter-length pictures, you need only pull the paper down behind your model. For full-length pictures, you should pull it down and across the floor in a gentle curve that disguises the ugly join between floor and wall. When you have your background paper in this position, take care not to walk on it yourself unless you remove your shoes. It tears and marks very easily, spoiling what could be an otherwise perfect picture.

Here, too, lighting can be kept simple, using an ordinary hand flashgun with reflectors around the model.

Some of the most unlikely areas around the home can become backgrounds and props for glamour photography.

A plain wall can be used in the home to make a background. In this instance, the seat has been used to mask the awkward join between the wall and floor.

If the pose isn't to be
full-length, there's no
need for the background
to reach the floor, as long
as it covers the area seen
by the camera.

A SIMPLE BACKGROUND

SUCCESSFUL GLAMOUR PHOTOGRAPHY

LIGHTING THE PROFESSIONAL WAY

While many pictures can be taken with basic, amateur lighting and background materials, there are some that are far better taken with professional gear, and others still that could *only* have been taken in the professional studio. These two shots are prime examples of the sort of pictures that *look* as though they might have been taken in a small, amateur studio but which, in reality, require the resources of a proper studio. In each case, the lighting would have caused difficulties for the amateur.

Two basic lights have been used for the picture of the girl with the shoe and mouse: one to the front, quite near the camera, and a second directly behind the model, arranged so that she blocks it from the camera. This second light has been fitted with a red gel to shed a glow on her hair and to match the colour of the shoe, as well as her costume. To make the effect work as well as this, the model must be posed a good way in front of the background, and when you add that distance to the distance between the model and the camera, you are into a shot that could be put together only in a sizeable studio. In a normal room, converted for the purpose, there just would not be enough space.

Lighting also plays its part in the second shot. Two lights have been used on the model herself, from each side and each masked to isolate its effect on particular areas of her body. The completely shadowless background has been provided by a large sheet of perspex with more light some way behind and shining through it. Again, the sheer size of studio needed for that set-up, plus the professional lighting gear needed for the effects on the model's body, puts what at first seems a simple shot firmly in the professional class.

The lighting looks fairly simple, but in fact it needed a large, professional studio to make it work effectively.

Once again, the lighting
appears straightforward,
but only a professional
studio could have
provided the evenness of
tone on the background.

LIGHTING THE PROFESSIONAL WAY

PROFESSIONALS' PROPS

Sometimes it's the props used for a picture which put it in the professional domain: props like the video-cameras used for this commercial picture by Jon Gray. A picture like this typifies the world of the professional photographer who shoots pictures for specific markets that the amateur photographer would rarely dream of and, when it comes right down to it, would have little need for.

The second picture is one that, on the surface, seems fairly straightforward, but which is in fact a very professional set-up. The girl has been posed in front of the sort of large-scale background that is rarely found in an amateur studio, and stood on a box covered with black velvet. In the original picture, there is a small wind-machine between her feet, responsible for blowing her skirt out in such an effective way. Few amateur photographers have access to props like this; fewer still would be able to make the wind-machine disappear in the final shot. That has been done, not photographically, but by a professional retouch artist – just one more service that the professional photographer regularly calls upon to turn out top-class pictures.

A simple enough shot on the face of it, but it needed a wind-machine placed at the model's feet, and then a professional retouching artist to remove the machine from the final picture.

A typical commercial shot that only a professional photographer would undertake.

PROFESSIONALS' PROPS

WHICH LIGHT FOR WHAT

While tungsten light is still used for certain specialist work, lighting in most modern photographic studios is provided by flash. Not the small, portable guns that are attached to cameras, but large, professional units on stands, run from the mains to give high light output and extra-fast recycling times. Waiting for the flash to recycle can break concentration on the part of the photographer and the model.

Sometimes a light is fitted to a boom – a long, counter-weighted arm from the top of a stand that can be used to shine light from overhead on to the model without the problems of the lighting stand itself appearing in the picture area. The quality of the light supplied by the basic flash unit is controlled in a number of ways. It might be shone through a honeycomb (a wide, criss-cross grid that softens the light) or through a snoot (a conical device that concentrates the beam into a hard, sharp spot). Both these accessories attach directly to the front of the flash unit.

More often than not, the flash is either reflected from a brolly, or shone through a thin diffuser. Both give a soft light that reduces the harshness of the shadows on the model's features. A brolly is umbrella-shaped and is usually lined on its inside surface with one of three colours. It can be plain white, when it gives an effect similar to that provided by the diffuser, or it might be silver to give a large, hard light, or gold to give a lovely warm glow to the model's skin tones.

Studio flash, softened by bouncing into a brolly, is used in most professional studios today. This picture is a typical example of the shadow-less effect such lighting provides.

As well as the usual lighting for the face, a top light has been used for this picture to give a little extra life to the girl's headgear.

Diffused flash was used for this picture – as is evident from the reflections on the beach ball.

SUCCESSFUL GLAMOUR PHOTOGRAPHY

WHICH LIGHT FOR WHAT

A SIMPLE SET-UP

A standard and simple lighting set-up for a glamour portrait needs to contain no more than three lights, each of which has its own effect.

First, there is the main light, sometimes known as the *keylight*. This will be soft, usually bounced from a reflector or brolly situated to one side and slightly above head height. The side it falls on should be the direction in which the model will mostly be looking. The main light gives shape to the face and features, but casts shadows to one side. It is the light which most affects exposure.

The second light, which is known as the *fill*, is used to soften the shadows produced by the main light. It will usually be used through a diffuser and its intensity will be less than that of the main light, so that the modelling is not completely destroyed.

The third light is known as the *catchlight* and it is used to add highlights to the hair. It will be harder than the other two and usually be directed from overhead through a snoot, a device that concentrates the beam on one particular area.

If necessary, a fourth light can also be used on the background to lighten it, to kill shadows of the model cast by the other lights, or to add an effect of its own. A coloured gel can be placed over this light to give a different effect to the background.

Reflectors can also be used in the lighting set-up. A common position for one is just below the model, out of camera range, to bounce a little extra light back into her eyes or into areas of her face shadowed by her hair.

Standard frontal lighting plus a little from above lift the darkness of the model's hair.

Predominant side-lighting has highlighted the model's features.

Diffused light from the front, plus strong lighting from the rear and to the left give a halo to the model's hair and texture to the rug.

A SIMPLE SET-UP

THE MOBILE STUDIO

Lighting for an obvious studio shot is, by its very nature, false: no natural light would ever provide the perfection of main light, fill, and catchlight. Move from the studio to a real location – the interior of a café, swimming pool, bedroom, bathroom, etc. – and things change. In order to light the model and her surroundings satisfactorily, the actual lighting set-up will often be every bit as false as it was in the studio, but here it must be made to *look* perfectly natural.

The experienced glamour photographer soon learns that natural-looking lighting is rarely, if ever, produced by natural light. That's why, when Jon Gray goes on location, he takes his studio with him! Not the whole lot of course, but two or three flash heads, brollies and reflectors with lighting stands that he knows he can use to create exactly the type of lighting effect he needs, whatever the location.

Sometimes natural light and studio light are combined and balanced to give atmosphere to a picture.

What looks like natural light rarely is. The professional takes a studio flash outfit with him for locations like this.

Again, simple studio lighting has been used in the home to emulate the effect of natural light.

THE MOBILE STUDIO

INSIDE STORY

Using flash to make an interior location appear to be lit naturally is an art in itself. Very often the rooms being used have their own forms of lighting which, while inadequate for photographic use, can be included to give extra atmosphere to the shot. Take, as an example, a bedroom with bedside lamps. A large, diffused flash head at the end of the bed shining back at the model will look natural because the light appears to be coming into the room as if through a window. The model on the bed would be lit well enough by this single flash, but the rest of the room would then fall into shadow. This actually happens in normal rooms lit by windows, but our eyes tend to adapt for differences in lighting levels and not notice them. Film and the camera lens aren't nearly so adaptable. So another flash might be placed on the floor, on the opposite side of the bed out of view of the camera, to shine up and around the far wall. A reflector might be added beside the camera to put some detail back into the bed on the camera side. Using a flash meter, the various levels around the room can then be read and adjusted on the flash heads until they balance. As a final touch, those bedside lamps can be switched on and, instead of using the usual flash synch speed, an exposure of as much as one second might be given. That way, detail in the room and on the model will be recorded by the combination of flash and the camera's aperture, while the longer-than-usual shutter speed will record the slight effect of the bedside lamps. And because the film is balanced for flash and daylight, rather than for the tungsten light from the lamps, they add a warm atmosphere to a shot that might otherwise have looked cold and clinical.

A picture like this needs to be lit by flash, but it has been balanced with natural light which contributes its own mood to the shot.

Natural light streaming through the net curtains would not be enough to light the model satisfactorily, so a small flash head has been used to fill the shadowed side of her body without overpowering the effect of the daylight.

DRAMATIC EFFECTS

For most studio shots, in which the lighting is subordinate to the actual pose, the straightforward main light, fill and catch set-up is quite adequate. But lighting can also be used more dramatically, to become an essential element in the picture's composition and even to enhance and to dominate the pose itself.

One of the easiest ways of creating a more dramatic effect is to introduce more back lighting. Moving a light round so that it shines on to the model at an angle from behind, rather than in front, draws a rim of brightness around her profile on the side of the light. Using two lights, one on each side, will produce a rim on *each* side of her body. The effect is taken to extremes when the light is moved directly behind the model, so that she blocks it from shining straight into the camera lens. The effect is unlike that produced by any other form of lighting. Shining through her hair, a dramatic halo of light is produced whose colour can be varied with coloured gels and whose effect is exaggerated with more elaborate hairstyles.

A different type of dramatic lighting can be had by throwing the major part of the picture into shadow and then highlighting one pertinent part of the model's features with a small area of light. Such a small area of light can be produced by using a snoot (as mentioned earlier) or barndoors which fit on to the front of the lighting unit and take the form of four flaps, two horizontal and two vertical, that close across its beam. They can then be opened in conjunction with one another to produce different 'shapes' of light, highlighting certain areas, while throwing those immediately adjacent into shadow. More sophisticated than either barndoors or snoot is the focusing spot which uses lenses like those in a projector to focus a spot of light actually on the subject. It can also be used to project cut-out shapes of light and even transparencies on to the model's body.

Strong lighting on the background itself kills shadows and isolates the model against it.

A snoot used over the flash will project a small beam of light that can be used to highlight a specific part of the model, while the adjacent areas fall into shadow.

Lighting mainly from the
rear rims the model with
a hard, dramatic light.

DRAMATIC EFFECTS

STUDIO SETS

Simplicity is the keynote in Jon Gray's studio sets. The simplest background is supplied by rolls of coloured paper that can be pulled down behind the model to give different effects, and Jon has found several ways of using these. Used straight, they make good, seamless backgrounds for a pose, whether it be head and shoulders, three-quarter or full-length. A variation is to paint the paper. Using an ordinary aerosol, Jon will spray a random pattern on the background in a colour that matches or contrasts with the base paper, then shoot his model a little way in front of the background so that the mottled pattern is thrown out of focus. Another variation is to cut the paper to make a large hole and a frame, then pose the model *behind* the background.

Coloured wire netting makes another 'background' that actually works well in front of the model, as do lengths of bamboo tied together to make a cage-like set with the model posed behind it. Louvre doors are a simple and versatile alternative for set building. Jon has several on hand and is continually painting them different colours to match the mood of the picture he has in mind.

A set built in the studio is, by its very nature, false. For glamour photography, studio sets are used to suggest rather than accurately depict a location. The set is there to enhance the pose, to act purely in a supporting role to the model. The minute the set begins to dominate the shot, its effectiveness is lost.

A simple background provided by a couple of red-painted louvre doors.

Sometimes the 'background' can be used in front of the model.

The background should
enhance a pose, never
dominate it.

STUDIO SETS

FILM TESTS

The market for a professional glamour photographer is wide, but the actual requirements are narrow: the vast majority of clients wants large-format colour transparencies.

Jon uses professional stock rollfilm. Unlike the standard film on sale in the average photo store, professional stock is available in specially tested batches, each with its own speed rating. A film speed designated, for instance, as 64 ASA, might actually be anything between 50 ASA and 80 ASA. To the professional, small differences like that can make the difference between an acceptably exposed picture and one that is slightly under- or over-exposed. So Jon checks and exposes accordingly. As a double-check, he runs a test on each photo session. That is, one

film from a batch is shot for each lighting set-up, then kept aside and processed in advance of the rest. Any small discrepancies in exposure can then be compensated for in processing the main batch of film.

Jon also uses a lot of Polaroid instant film – not in a Polaroid camera, but in a special back that fits to his normal camera. With that he checks angles, poses, lighting and even exposure in advance, making subtle changes and shooting again. When it looks right on the Polaroid, it can be committed to transparency film. At one time the use of Polaroids was considered to be something of a cheat. Today, it's seen as an invaluable aid to improving results and saving film.

One magazine is kept throughout a location shoot as a test film with each pose and location numbered. Back home, this film is processed in advance of the rest and, if need be, the processing of the main batch is then adjusted accordingly.

FILM TESTS

For a calendar shoot, it's sometimes necessary to include more than just the model in the picture: the client may well want his name seen too.

Another shot, very much in the typical calendar mould.

1983

APRIL   MAY   JUNE

1983

JULY	AUGUST	SEPTEMBER

A subtler form of
advertising for the client,
with his motif displayed
on the model's hat.
Integrating the
commercial aspect with
the glamour pose is all
part of the photographer's
job.

Can you spot the plug for
the client? It's on more
than the hat.

1983

NOVEMBER	DECEMBER	JANUARY

CALENDAR GIRLS

THE GLAMOUR PHOTOGRAPHER AT WORK

ORGANIZING A CALENDAR SHOOT

A calendar shoot, such as those for which Jon Gray is famous, starts with the client. He will make the initial approach with a proposal for the type of product he is looking for. Once he has an agreement from the photographer, the client appoints a creative director for the project. He's the man who comes up with the basic theme for the calendar. He will often have artists' roughs drawn up for the type of poses he visualizes being used and presents these to the client for approval.

Once the initial idea has been approved, a suitable location will be chosen, girls interviewed for the job and arrangements made for travel and accommodation. These latter arrangements are largely left to the client, and the photographer organizes the models and the more artistic side of the trip. From this point on, the success or failure of the venture is down to him: the buck finally stops with the photographer. It's his experience that finds the right girls for the trip, organizes the equipment that will be needed and makes sure everyone and everything gets to the right location at the right time.

On a calendar shoot, the choice of models will largely be left to the experience of the photographer, who picks girls that he knows will best suit the chosen location.

A calendar shoot usually involves at least two girls and, in making a choice, the photographer will try to contrast a blonde with a brunette.

THE GLAMOUR PHOTOGRAPHER AT WORK

ORGANIZING A CALENDAR SHOOT

GOING PLACES

The choice of the right girls for a calendar shoot is second only to the choice of the right location. Foreign countries are used so often for two reasons: first, the photographer knows he can rely on the weather; and second, an exotic location adds to the element of fantasy that is so important in this type of work. No one wants to look at grey skies and mundane surroundings in glamour photography.

Locations are chosen to match the theme of the calendar and to comply with the available budget. Once a location has been decided upon, a professional glamour photographer like Jon Gray will research as much as he can at home. He will rarely visit a location without knowing something about the country. He uses guide and travel books, along with any pictures of the location that can be found, to assess its potential. Its climate will be researched to discover at what time of year the weather will be most suitable. Just as important are the country's laws and religion, and its political stability. Any one of these things can create massive problems for the photographer who chooses a location without doing his research. Finding the right place means a lot more than merely looking for lush backgrounds and tropical weather.

Foreign locations are most often chosen for calendar shoots because of their glamorous image, the element of fantasy they can add to the pictures and because the photographer knows he can rely on the weather.

GETTING THROUGH CUSTOMS

Getting equipment to a location can be a nightmare. Many countries demand that the photographer takes out a *carnet* – this is a declaration of the equipment that he is bringing into the country, which can then be checked as he is leaving. The main purpose is to make sure that the equipment is being brought in for use, and not for sale. If the photographer doesn't take out everything he brought in he could be in serious trouble. It is not unknown for airport officials in some countries to demand a deposit of as much as £5,000 on any equipment being brought in.

One of the biggest problems is the one that dogs all photographers, amateur or professional, that of the dreaded X-ray machines used at airports to check luggage for bombs or arms. The average amateur photographer, with only a few rolls of film to take out of the country, can ask for a hand search, and in many countries he will get cooperation. There are many places abroad, however, which simply refuse, and others still which are just plain awkward. On one occasion Jon was forced to open each of 350 boxes of film for a separate search before he was allowed to board a plane.

Lead-shielded bags designed to deflect X-rays are of little use, despite what the advertisements tell you. They will shield the film against low-dose X-rays but if officials in some countries see a lead-shielded object in luggage, they simply turn the X-ray dosage up to an all-time high so that they can determine its contents. This action often defeats the whole object.

Cases checked through as normal luggage for the aircraft hold are also X-rayed, but only randomly. The trick, Jon has found, is not to draw attention to your luggage. Putting film in large, sealed metal containers with *'Film Do Not X-ray'* plastered all over the sides, only leads to trouble. This is a sure-fire method of attracting attention and ensuring that your luggage will be chosen for the X-ray machines. Jon goes for the opposite approach. He packs his film in a firm, but fairly shabby suitcase, the sort of innocuous-looking case that might be used by tourists travelling on the same flight. Then he checks the case through baggage control in the normal way and hopes for the best. So far he has never had a film damaged by X-ray fogging.

Getting a picture like this relies on a lot more than the photographer and the model being on form. It starts with what sometimes seems the impossible task of getting all the necessary equipment to the location.

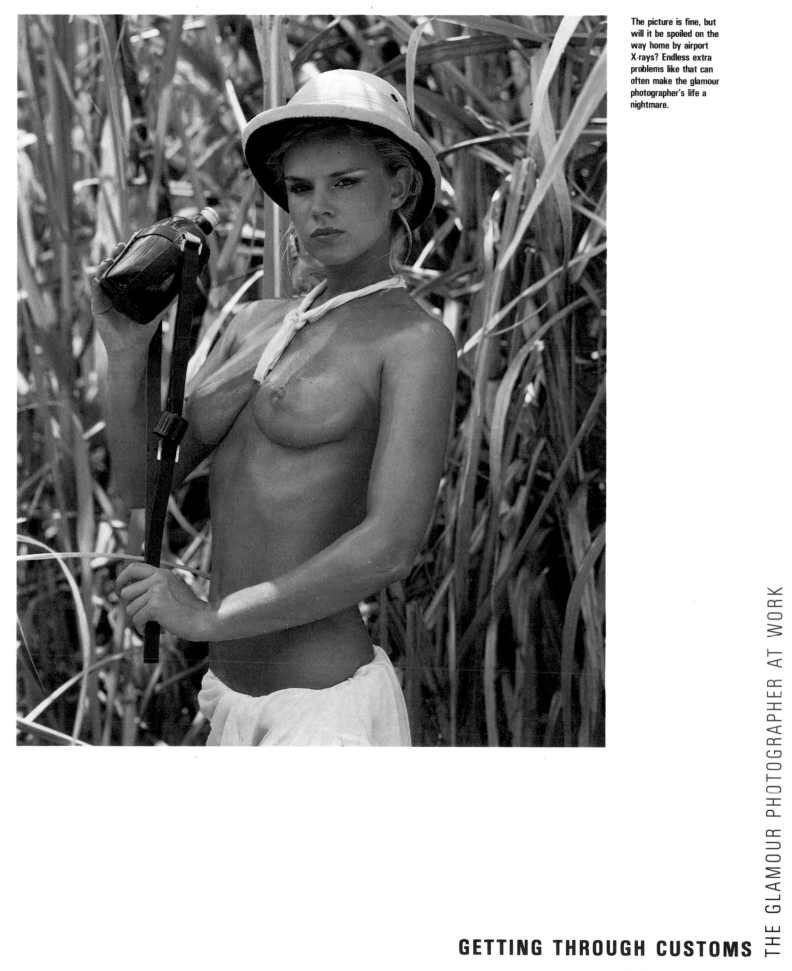

The picture is fine, but will it be spoiled on the way home by airport X-rays? Endless extra problems like that can often make the glamour photographer's life a nightmare.

GETTING THROUGH CUSTOMS THE GLAMOUR PHOTOGRAPHER AT WORK

THE TAN'S THE THING

Sometimes, when the budget is high, the photographer and art director will fly to the chosen country in advance to scout out locations. More often, the whole team will fly out together. The average shoot will last two weeks, including around ten days' shooting. For the first few days, photographer and models part company.

If he has not already done so, the photographer will travel around looking for locations, while the models make their own preparations for the shoot. This is when they tan up. At one time it was common to see pictures of a topless model with a deep, rich tan and unattractive pale marks where her bikini top had been. These days, no professional model would dare to arrive for a shoot in that condition. Tans must be all-over. So they sunbathe topless, wearing nothing more than the briefest of G-strings.

Again, this is an area where the professional must know her own body to the full. She must know what types of oil she can use to aid the tan, how to tan evenly all over without any patchy areas and how to tan without burning. She must know when to lie in the sun and when to move into the shade. She often has only a few days to turn her pale skin tones into the rich, golden brown so beloved of glamour photographers. In this business, even sunbathing is an art that must be learned and applied in a totally professional way.

A deep, rich tan all over is essential for today's glamour photography, and very often the model only has a couple of days at the very start of the trip to get it exactly right.

THE TAN'S THE THING

THE OTHER SIDE OF THE CAMERA

You hear a lot about glamour photography from the photographer's side, but rarely does anyone ask the model how she feels about it all. What *is* it like from her side of the camera?

One thing that all models agree on is that the job is hard work – a lot harder than most people seem to think. People will tell you that it's glamorous work, that models get the chance to travel the world and see places that their friends of the same age might never even hope to see, and that compared to other jobs it's very well paid. But against that must be set the facts that the girls have little time for sight-seeing in the marvellous places they visit and their working life is a lot shorter than even the average dancer's. They must make as much money as they can while they have the chance, in the sure knowledge that they will be retiring by the time they are twenty-five.

Because of light conditions, very little outdoor glamour photography is carried out around midday, most of the work being done in the early morning and late afternoon, perhaps stretching a little into the early evening. So the girls must be prepared for early starts, on location, made-up and smiling as early as 6 a.m. Late nights are out, too, not just because they must get up early, but because too much nightlife can quickly affect their looks. The last thing the client wants to see when he is choosing glamour pictures for his calendar is dark bags under the model's eyes.

Stripping off for a picture means nothing to the professional model. It is, she will tell you, no worse than undressing for the doctor. It's why she's there, it's what she's getting paid for, it's her job.

Posing works in different ways with different photographers. Models will tell you that some have very definite ideas of exactly what they want and are unwilling to deviate. These photographers don't want to listen to the models' ideas and can be downright rude, telling the girls to do as they're told. Such working relationships rarely lead to the relaxed atmosphere that is necessary for top glamour photography. Jon Gray is far more casual in his approach. He is open to suggestions from his models, and he earns their respect on this account. Most poses start with his ideas, but girls who have worked with him will tell you that he is always prepared to listen and to try out *their* ideas as well. Cooperation is the name of the game, and when the model works *with* the photographer rather than just *for* him, the results will always be better.

Sitting in the sun, looking glamorous, might seem like an easy way to earn a living, but any truly professional model will tell you that it's actually a lot of hard work.

Some photographers dictate exactly the type of pose they want and the model isn't allowed to deviate from it. Jon Gray prefers to allow his model a say in the pose; they'll tell you that he is always ready to listen to their ideas.

THE GLAMOUR PHOTOGRAPHER AT WORK

THE OTHER SIDE OF THE CAMERA

SPREADING THE COSTS

Travel is an expensive business. Working for a large corporation where money is no object makes life easy for the whole crew. But, very often, the budget doesn't stretch to the requirements. Rather than cut back and use a less expensive background for the pictures, other ways must be found to reduce the cost of the trip. Airlines with interests in hotels are very cooperative. Often they will give concessions on air fares and hotel accommodation for no more than a credit or mention in the publication for which the photographer is working. That, in turn, has to be agreed with the client before proceeding. Travel companies are similarly approachable for the same sort of concessions in exchange for what is, in essence, a free advertisement for their organization.

The photographer can off-set some of his expenses by linking up with a picture agency, offering them pictures for their files on his return from the trip. The original client has the first pick of the transparencies but, with so much being shot and comparatively little being used for the calendar itself, there will always be a lot of other pictures left over. The picture agency must undertake not to sell pictures similar to those being used on the calendar to a competitive market, but there is a wealth of other markets which use glamour and which will come to the agency for their requirements. That way, from one calendar shoot, the photographer might find his pictures also being used in travel brochures, on magazine covers, record sleeves, even greetings cards. It all helps to defray the initial cost of the trip.

Very often, ways must be found to help spread the cost of a location shoot. So, while the photographer gives prime importance to shooting for his client, he will also shoot pictures like this one for himself, using them later as stock shots to be put into an agency or even to illustrate a book such as this.

SPREADING THE COSTS

GETTING A BIT FLASH

Jon uses a lot of different equipment on a shoot, but four particular pieces are always around: the camera, of course, and a tripod, but he nearly always adds to these a large reflector and a powerful, heavy-duty flashgun.

The glamour photographer rarely works with the sun directly behind him; more often it is to the side or behind the model, and in those conditions the reflector is used to bounce light back into the shadowed areas of the model's features. Unfolded, it can be as large as 8-ft square, with different surfaces used for different effects: soft, hard or warm, according to its colour.

The flashgun, sometimes used on the camera but more often fitted on its own stand to the side, is used for two purposes: to balance the light on the model with that on the background, and to give an extra sparkle to her eyes.

On a shaded veranda, a straight shot of the model would produce no more than a silhouette against a brightly-lit background. With a flashgun adjusted to give around a quarter of the light falling on the background from the sun, a far more natural effect would be achieved. The flash will light the model's features in a way that appears to be perfectly natural, while the sun will illuminate the background and give highlights to the model's hair. A higher intensity of flash, actually balancing its light with the level of the background illumination, would totally destroy the required atmosphere.

Shooting in the shade of a tree, a powerful flashgun is often used to fill the shadows with what, in the final picture, appears to be natural light.

A large reflector is a useful alternative to a flashgun for bouncing light back into the model's face, giving a soft light that complements her pose and expression.

GETTING A BIT FLASH

SHOOTING IN THE FOREST

Glamour photography, on location at least, seems at times to be inextricably concerned with sun, sand and sea. Yet inland, away from the beach, there are just as many locations, many of which don't present half the technical problems involved with shooting around sand and water.

Trees make wonderful backdrops for several reasons. In the tropics at least, their trunks can take on interesting shapes and colours, offering rough textures that contrast well with the smooth lines of the model's body. Lush, rich foliage can be used as a straightforward background, or as something with which to surround the model. (Care must be taken by the photographer working this way, in case the green of the leaves sheds a cast on the model's skin tones. A little fill-in flash here can usually be relied on to kill the cast and render skin the correct colour.) Tropical fruit and flowers from the trees make interesting accessories for the model to work with or hold.

The direct, harsh light of midday is largely impractical for glamour photography, but move your model into the shade of a tree and the session can be continued even when the sun is directly overhead. When the sun is shining through gaps in the leaves, it can dapple the model's body with intricate patterns of light and shade. Thicker foliage will act as a filter, softening harsh light and making it far more suitable for the subject. Alternatively, exposures can be adjusted for the brightly-lit background outside the tree's shadow and the model lit with reflectors or a little fill-in flash.

Glamour photography needn't be exclusively concerned with sun, sand and sea. Inland, trees and shrubs make effective backgrounds for the right types of poses.

In the tropics, foliage is large and lush, making a perfect foil for the glamour model.

SHOOTING IN THE FOREST

THE SURPRISE ELEMENT

Take an attractive girl with a beautiful body, put her on a sun-drenched beach and you are well on your way to successful glamour pictures. But you might also find those pictures lack a certain something. The technique is fine, the pose is perfect, but there is still something missing, the something that turns a good glamour picture into a great one. What is very often needed is an element of surprise.

A naked girl on a beach looks attractive, but not unusual. Nudity and beaches go together. Put the same girl in the same pose in a city street and a strong element of surprise is added. Taken to extremes the results can be corny and even ridiculous, but executed with taste and subtlety, the trick works well and lends a note of eroticism where it might previously have been lacking.

The same goes too for the use of props. Posed behind a fruit-seller's stall, in the window of a local hut, sitting by a camp fire, maybe – anything that is slightly out of the ordinary will add to the mood of the picture. The same is true of weather conditions and unusual times of day. Glamour photography is traditionally associated with bright sunlight. Pose your model in front of a colourful sunset or against a dramatically overcast sky and, again, the surprise element works its magic.

There is definitely something erotic about nudity in unexpected places and, providing a situation is not taken to laughable extremes, the glamour photographer can exploit that for yet another way of adding something a little different to his pictures.

Very often, it's the element of surprise that makes a picture successful. Nudity in unexpected places is particularly effective.

THE SURPRISE ELEMENT

CHANGING ANGLES

Viewpoint plays an important role in all photography, and our subject is no exception. It is the way you look at a location, and the way you look at the model. When Jon Gray is choosing a location, he looks at it from all sorts of different angles, not just from the traditional eye-level. Sometimes the most unpromising location can become something quite spectacular simply by a change of camera position. The interesting quay or harbour wall that is spoilt by a messy background of houses can be improved, for instance, by lowering the camera to ground-level. As the viewpoint is lowered, the background drops away until only the foreground is seen, isolated against the sky. The picture which looked fussy and confusing from eye-level suddenly turns into an ideal location.

The same is true of the model herself. No one has decreed that all glamour pictures must show every inch of the girl. Sometimes the full-length shot works well, other times a three-quarter-length picture works even better, and occasionally the really tight close-up on one particular part of her body gives the shot a dramatic impact that would have been impossible with the camera a few feet further back. It almost goes without saying that the chosen areas of the model's body must be perfect; but it is equally true that working this way allows you to use a model who might be less than perfect in other areas, ignoring her defects and concentrating your camera on her best points.

A glamour picture doesn't have to show the model's face.

A low camera angle has added its own effect to the model's unusual costume and pose.

Often, just one area of a model's body will give a far more evocative picture than would have been obtained by shooting a full-length pose.

A high viewpoint on to the model gives yet another variation on camera angle.

CHANGING ANGLES

OTHER PEOPLE'S HOUSES

Other people's homes can make interesting locations, either indoors or out. Looking for locations during his first few days abroad, Jon Gray always keeps an eye open for an impressive-looking house that he knows will make an interesting backdrop for his pictures. Shooting on private land without permission is naturally out, but a few inquiries and a polite request to use the house for a day are nearly always met with acceptance.

In the tropical countries where much of Jon's location work takes place, houses all have their individual looks, many with ornate exteriors and verandas which are perfect for positioning models on or against. Most big houses have their own land, too, where photographer and models can work in private, away from nosy passers-by.

Back home, house locations can also be found by reading property advertisements in glossy magazines. These can tell the photographer most of what he needs to know, especially when they show pictures both inside and outside the house. A few telephone calls are all it takes to find an owner who is agreeable to hiring out his property for a day for what, to him, will seem an unusual and exciting purpose. To photographer and model, it is just another location to add its own individual atmosphere to a picture.

Shooting from inside the room, out on to a balcony has made an unusual setting and location.

Reading property advertisements can sometimes lead a photographer to an interesting location and the chance to shoot in a real room, rather than having to build an elaborate set in the studio.

A very feminine bedroom has been enhanced by the use of a little soft focus.

OTHER PEOPLE'S HOUSES

ALL AROUND THE HOUSE

Indoors, large houses can provide different and unusual locations for glamour work. The most obvious rooms are bathroom and bedroom, both of which are traditionally associated with nudity, but just as effective are other areas, attractive simply because they are *not* usually associated with a naked girl. The impressive staircase down to a large baronial hall; the snugness of a well-furnished lounge with a roaring fire in the grate; a kitchen that can contain the warmth of old-fashioned wooden units, or the coldness of ultra-modern kitchenware – they all make interesting backgrounds, and can add that element of surprise that lifts the picture right out of the ordinary.

Working in houses, rather than in studio sets designed to look like houses, can restrict camera angles through having to shoot in cramped conditions. In a studio, you can take the camera back as far as you like within reason; in a real house, you soon find yourself bumping into walls as you step back to compose the picture better. One trick that Jon Gray uses to help him out of that problem is to shoot into a mirror. A large one can be used for two distinct purposes. In the first, you can make it obvious what you are doing, using the mirror itself as a frame for your picture; in the second, you can move in closer so that the camera angle doesn't take in the edges of the mirror, and so appears to be giving a perfectly straightforward view. All the mirror has done in this latter instance is effectively add length or width to the room. Because a reflection is, in theory, as far *behind* the mirror as the actual object of that reflection is in front, focusing can be adjusted to a setting that totals the camera-to-mirror distance *plus* the mirror-to-subject distance. Used intelligently, then, a large, good quality mirror can effectively double the size of a room.

Looking over a house for possible picture potential, a piece of furniture like this would be recorded on instant film as a reminder of what's available.

Having found an interesting prop, the model begins to work with it. This picture is from a Polaroid test shot.

Finally, the finished picture is set up and shot, combining model and location in just the right way.

Bedrooms are among the
more obvious rooms used
for glamour photography.

ALL AROUND THE HOUSE

TRICKS OF THE TRADE

Things aren't always what they seem. Sometimes the most natural-looking picture has taken a lot of contrivance. In the studio, such shots are often a matter of course and part of their attraction is this very contrivance; outdoors, the photographer's fiddles shouldn't be so obvious.

The girl who is standing in a banana grove, casually holding some fruit that hangs from the nearby branches of a tree might actually have been far too short for a straight shot and, in all probability, she is standing on a metal camera box out of shot. The bush in the background covered with colourful blooms of just the right number and colour, in exactly the right position, may well be the work of the photographer's assistant who has cut the flowers from another bush and put them in position. Behind the model and slightly out of focus, the trick will never be detected. The magnificent conch shell

that the model appears to have found on the beach was probably bought specially for the picture the night before in a local souvenir shop.

And of course there are numerous technical tricks of the trade that should never be evident in the finished picture: the fill-in flash used beside the camera to give a lighting effect that looks more appropriate than that produced by natural light; the reflectors that fill dark shadows that would otherwise look unattractive; the filters that warm up a model's sometimes pale skin tones; the out-of-shot white umbrella that has been used to diffuse and soften the sun's harsh light.

In glamour photography, the end result might look perfectly natural, but it is far from unusual for the photographer to help things along a little with a few well-tried tricks. The end justifies the means – but only when the means are not evident in the end.

The pose and the lighting couldn't look more natural, but what's going on behind the scenes?

The truth behind the
illusion, as Jon Gray sets
up the picture on the
opposite page.

TRICKS OF THE TRADE

THE GLAMOUR PHOTOGRAPHER AT WORK

WATER, WATER EVERYWHERE

Water makes one of the most natural backgrounds for glamour photography, simply because we associate it generally with being undressed. The sea, a river, a waterfall, they all make wonderful locations which your model can pose against or become involved with. These locations can range from an ordinary beach such as you might find in any holiday resort, to the more exotic atmosphere of a waterfall in a tropical forest.

Water is always on the move and use can be made of that movement. Pose your model against the edge of the sea and let the waves roll over her. Materials like cheesecloth become transparent as they get wet and can be used to add an erotic element to the picture.

Use fast shutter speeds and water will be frozen into individual droplets. Pose your model in the water and have her leap up, throwing spray as she moves, then catch the shot with a fast speed. Alternatively, use slow speeds and the water takes on a soft, fluffy appearance. Persuade your model to sit under a waterfall and she will appear to be bathed in a mass of tumbling cotton-wool.

A large expanse of water acts as a gigantic reflector and so light, which might otherwise have too much contrast, will be flattened into a far more pleasing quality, unique to these particular surroundings.

Textures produced by water on skin can make for strongly sensual pictures, enhanced if the model has a dark skin tone. To add to the effect, ask her to rub in some baby oil. It will give a glistening surface to the skin and, because oil naturally repels water, it will force the water to form into individual droplets or rivulets that stand out strongly against a dark skin.

Remember that substances like sand adhere to wet skin. That can present problems to certain types of shots, but it can also be used to advantage in others, the sand clinging to the model's body, adding the surprise element of a rough texture in place of the usual smoothness. If you are shooting pictures like this, however, always remember the comfort of your model. Sand can be irritating, so don't shoot for too long before allowing her to wash it off.

Water makes a perfect backdrop for glamour photography, its appearance and texture changing with each new direction of light.

A large expanse of water
can act like a gigantic
reflector, giving the
photographer a different
sort of lighting on his
model's body.

WATER, WATER EVERYWHERE

MESSING ABOUT IN BOATS

There's something exotic about boats. From large, sea-going yachts down to the smallest dinghy, they represent something owned only by a minority and so are often the subject of envy and fantasy. It's that very element of fantasy that makes them so suitable for glamour photography.

On location, boat owners can usually be persuaded to lend their services to a glamour photographer, if for no other reason, for the opportunity of spending a day in the company of a couple of beautiful naked girls. Owners usually take

a pride in their boats, so they are clean and brightly painted, offering a wealth of backgrounds for poses: lying lazily on the deck, at the wheel, working on the rigging of a yacht. Below decks, boats provide unusual props found nowhere else: brass lamps, richly polished woodwork, portholes.

Working on a boat also gives you the advantage of privacy. Move no more than a few yards from the quay and you are cut off in a world of your own, where you can work uninterrupted.

Working on a boat, rather than just beside it, can give the photographer and model a whole host of new props to play with.

The interesting structure of the boat makes it ideal for inclusion in glamour shots by the sea.

MESSING ABOUT IN BOATS

ON THE ROCKS

Rocks are sharp, jagged and hard. They make an effective contrast to the soft, gentle curves of a glamour model. Because rocks are irregularly formed, they can suggest poses and shapes for your model to follow, as she moulds herself with the contours, blending, harmonizing and contrasting with the surface. Close to the sea, some rocks are worn down by the tide to a smooth, round shape that makes a further foil for the shape or form of your model.

You can use rocks to pose your model on a viewpoint higher than that of the camera, giving you the chance to set her against the sky with no other background intruding. Conversely, they can be used by the photographer himself to get a higher viewpoint and so shoot down at the model lying full-length on the sand beneath. A viewpoint such as this is useful if circumstances force you to shoot around the middle of the day. Normally, lighting is at its best in the early morning or late afternoon; midday gives a harsh top light, throwing eyes into dark pools of shadow that can be very unattractive. Getting above your model and shooting down at her lying on the ground turns the situation on its side, lighting her evenly from above. Working this way on a beach, Jon Gray will pose a dark-skinned model against the white of the sand or, in places like Tenerife, famous for its black volcanic sand, a pale-skinned blonde makes a marvellous contrast with the natural background.

Working in a location like this last one, experimenting with exposures can give different results: over-exposing will give more detail to the sand while paling the model's skin tones; under-exposing will darken skin tones, while turning the sand jet black.

Shadows across the sand have helped break up the glaring brightness that can often spoil a picture like this.

The harshness of rocks
makes a perfect foil for
the smooth lines of the
model's body.

ON THE ROCKS THE GLAMOUR PHOTOGRAPHER AT WORK

THE OTHER TYPE OF EXPOSURE

No particularly specialized equipment is needed for shooting around beaches and water, although a warm-up filter such as an 81A or 81B can be useful. These are a pale straw colour and combat the blueness of the light caused by reflections from the sea.

The way you *use* your equipment, however, does vary slightly from the way it might be used inland. Exposure techniques have to be particularly watched. A beach and the sea will reflect far more light than the normal ground and so exposures might be adversely affected. A normal meter reading, taken over the average scene will over-react to the brightness and so give a reading that will lead to under-exposure. It is usually necessary to open up by one or two stops to compensate.

In most glamour photography, it's the model's skin tones that are the most important and so, for safety's sake, readings should be taken close-up and then adhered to, no matter what the camera's meter might be suggesting at the moment the shutter is pressed.

Camera exposures need to be watched carefully when shooting on beaches and near the sea. It's important that the model's skin tones record correctly.

Shooting in open shade
helps to combat the
problem caused by too
much light reflected from
sand and sea.

THE OTHER TYPE OF EXPOSURE

THE GLAMOUR PHOTOGRAPHER AT WORK

CAMERA CARE

Working on beaches and near water, camera gear is in permanent danger, and the photographer is wise to remember that.

Sand is notorious for getting into mechanisms and jamming up the works, so never lay a camera down on the beach. When not in use, keep all equipment in a dust-proof metal box, preferably wrapped individually in plastic bags.

Whenever he changes a film magazine or lens, Jon Gray can be seen squirting a blast of compressed air around the inner surfaces to blow out any grit that might have found its way in. He uses the same technique at the end of every day's shooting by the sea to keep his equipment in the best possible condition.

Water is corrosive – and sea water is the worst of all. A permanent watch must be kept on all equipment for the slightest signs of rust. The professional uses a tripod for much of his work, and that includes when he is knee-deep in the sea or a swimming pool. To protect the legs of his tripod from rust, Jon takes the simple and inexpensive precaution of tying waterproof plastic bin liners around the feet.

The location looks lovely in the photograph, but it is a potential danger to the camera. The photographer must be continually on his guard against possible damage to equipment in locations like this.

After a day's shooting by the sea, the photographer will check his camera thoroughly for the slightest sign of rust. Sea water is one of the most corrosive hazards around.

The equipment costs thousands, but where would it be without plastic bin liners to protect it from the water?

CAMERA CARE THE GLAMOUR PHOTOGRAPHER AT WORK

A CAUTIONARY TALE

Sometimes the most unexpected problems arise, which have nothing to do with models, posing or equipment. The shoot that seems to be going well until the model is suddenly conscious of a score of grinning men leering at her from the undergrowth is just one classic and fairly common problem that has to be coped with.

Jon Gray tells a story of the day he decided to pose his model a little way offshore in a boat that just happened to be handy. He dragged it into the water, unaware that the bung was out and, within minutes, it had sunk. From nowhere, it seemed, the owner arrived, complete with a dangerous-looking machete and a demand for the equivalent of £50. Jon had only about half that amount of cash on him. He offered to drag the boat out of the sea and empty it of water, but the owner wasn't to be placated. He had, he insisted, lost a day's fishing and he wanted compensation. Getting models and equipment into his nearby Land-rover as he negotiated the problem, Jon eventually took out all the cash he had, pushed it into the boat owner's hand and fled. Looking over his shoulder from a safe distance, he saw the owner dragging his boat from the water and emptying it ready for use. For him, at least, it had been an unexpected and highly profitable day.

If you don't want to land in trouble, it's a good idea to check that boat owners are aware of your intentions before you start to shoot.

Add a second model and the picture doubles its appeal.

A CAUTIONARY TALE

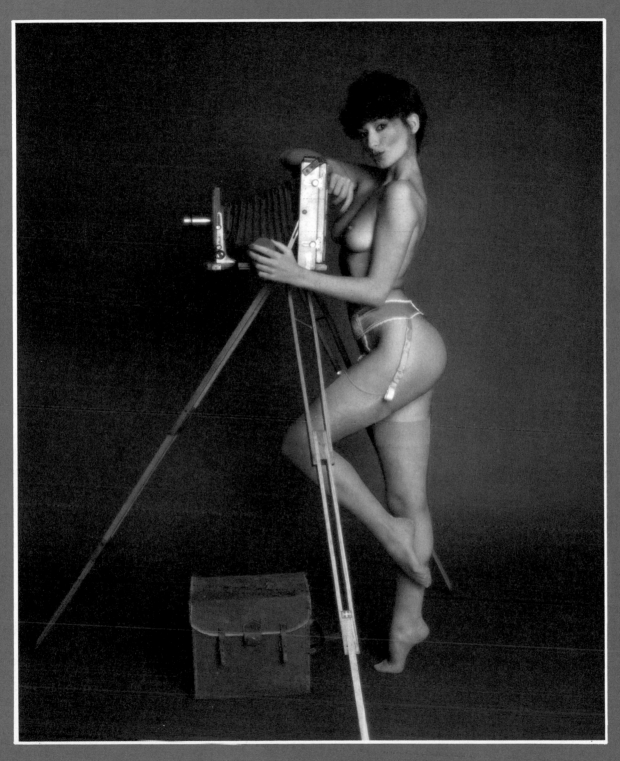

JUST ONE GIRL

Simplicity is the keynote in so much of Jon Gray's work, and this picture, he feels, epitomizes his way of working. Props, unless used with care, can detract from the mood of a picture and so here he has used none. Just one girl, in the barest and simplest of costumes, against an interesting background. The brown of her body and the greens of her surroundings blend perfectly and, to give the picture a little extra punch, he has added the yellow headband. Its colour alone stands out in the composition and draws the viewer's eye to the girl's face. The overall result is simple, but very effective.

This picture was taken for a calendar and, before the shoot, the client gave Jon two small toy trucks that he wanted to be included in at least one of the shots. Jon's task was to do this in an interesting and, he decided, slightly humorous way. Girls' bottoms, he knew, were not an original subject, but moving in close and adding the vehicles in this way gave an abstract view of the girls in a picture that is humorous, but still sexy. Again, simplicity of style and approach has played its part in the final effect.

A TOUCH OF HUMOUR

YOU DON'T HAVE TO BE BRILLIANT...

Just because a glamour photographer shoots in colour, he shouldn't feel obliged to fill the picture with every hue under the sun. Jon likes to subdue colours by shooting in the shade, and this is one of his favourite pictures, taken away from the brilliance of the tropical sun. He likes the muted tones, the way the background colours blend with one another, and the way the lower lighting level has allowed him to use a shutter speed that blurs the water, adding to the softness of the image. And yet, Jon is aware that no picture should appear *too* soft. Hence the small but very important addition of the flower to the girl's hair, adding a splash of colour that contrasts with the surroundings and, once again, draws the eye to the principal point of interest: the model herself.

YOU DON'T HAVE TO BE BRILLIANT...

Glamour photography is a lot more commonplace these days than it was just a few years ago, and it's getting to the point where it loses its effect simply because it is so much more readily accepted. One way around that problem is to introduce humour to the subject, something which has been handled to perfection in this, one of Jon's favourite commissions. The pictures were produced with comedian Les Dawson. The model was chosen not just for her glamorous looks, but also in this instance for her personality and ability to add a little acting talent to the pictures. Unlike many calendar shoots, the brief for this one was *very* tight. Every detail of each picture was planned in advance, then the two figures were shot in a studio against a white background, always in the positions they would be in in the finished picture. The artwork was added at the printing stage.

With so many commissions coming from the world of calendars, Jon enjoys getting work from the magazine market. *Amateur Photographer* is the world's best-selling weekly photographic magazine. Originally the magazine obtained some of Jon's work from his picture agency, but later commissioned pictures from him specifically for the magazine's cover. Here is a small selection that Jon feels worked especially well. The brief was to produce a set of pictures that were sexy, but not over-the-top, bearing in mind that he was shooting for a photographic magazine rather than for the real glamour market. He was asked to produce something creative, interesting photographically and with space, as all magazines need, for the title and the coverlines – the words that tell the reader what's inside. The brief sounded tight at first but, with creativity, Jon soon opened it up into a set of very different and remarkably appealing pictures, ideally suited to the magazine.

With Jon's dedication to simplicity, it's rare that he sets out to shoot an out-and-out special-effect picture. On the occasions when he does, he goes for the simplest means of creating the required effect. For this shot – another of his personal favourites – a sparkler was attached to a fan that revolved behind the model's head. A light with a blue gel behind the model added its tint to her hair.

SPECIAL EFFECTS

FAVOURITE LOCATIONS

Ask Jon to name his favourite location and he will immediately mention Jamaica. It has so many different moods that so suit the world of glamour photography. Streams, rivers, waterfalls, beaches, rocks, interiors, landscapes and of course the weather, all contribute to the perfect location for the glamour photographer. Jon has used Jamaica several times and has every intention of using it again. Every time he goes there, he says, he finds more locations than he can use. It's easy to travel around the island, the people are friendly and very often thc best picture possibilities are found no more than a stone's throw from the nearest road – so convenient for photographer and models alike.

Locations vary and, just as Jon loves
Jamaica for exterior shots, so he has
favourite locations for interiors. This
picture is another of his personal
favourites, shot in the London home of an
actor and found for Jon by Location
Finders, an agency that specializes in
seeking out places for photographers and
film crews to shoot. This particular house
was originally used because it had a
beautiful Victorian bathroom but, says Jon,
if one room is interesting, it's a fair bet that
others will be too and a quick look around
found this bedroom that could almost have
been designed with a glamour
photographer in mind.

BEDROOM SCENES

Every glamour photographer has a
favourite model, and Jon Gray is no
exception. Obviously, the type of girl he
favours is one who is glamorous with a
good body, but she must also have the
right personality to give a picture just that
little extra sparkle. She must be prepared
to work hard and often for long hours at a
time. She must be able to adapt to the
difference between shooting for a couple
of hours in the studio and working abroad
for a fortnight, Jon says. If he is to come
back with the pictures the client wants, he
must have a girl who can take the hard
work and come up smiling every time.

Here's the other side of glamour, a picture that could so easily have been tasteless, but with the sense of humour of the photographer and – most important of all – of the model herself, the picture forms just one of a whole series of winners. The model is an actress whom Jon originally met when he was commissioned by a poster company to shoot a humorous fat lady picture. Since then he has used the same model for a lot of different pictures, all on the same sort of theme. The original poster has been very successful, going into several reprints and the model remains one of Jon's favourite ladies.

GOING OVER BIG

THE BEST TIME OF DAY

When working on location, Jon shoots all day, moving into the shade when the sun is too high in the sky for successful pictures, but like most photographers concerned with this type of work, he will tell you that his favourite time is early evening. A similar light can be seen at dawn, but only for a brief time. On top of which, as Jon points out, no one is at his or her best working at four o'clock in the morning. In the early evening, it's different. In countries like Jamaica, the light can easily last for three or four hours up to around seven o'clock. The sun is warmer in colour than at midday, it is lower in the sky, giving catchlights to the eyes, but not so strong as to make the model squint. Skies at this time are moodier too. It's the most productive time of day for a glamour photographer and Jon's favourite time.

THE BEST TIME OF DAY

SIMPLE, SUBTLE AND SEXY

Ask Jon Gray to show you one picture
that he likes more than any other and
which he feels sums up his own style to
perfection, and he will return time and
time again to this one. He likes the picture
for its shape, its subtle lighting, the pose
which is sexy without being overtly so; but
on top of all this, he likes it for one factor
that, for him, is perhaps the most
important of all: he likes it for its sheer
simplicity.

SIMPLE, SUBTLE AND SEXY

CAUTION THESE SWITCHES MUST BE OFF IF NOT REQUIRED

MADE IN ENGLAND BY
STROBE EQUIPMENT LTD
LONDON

1000 J   2000 J   1000 J

OFF   A   OFF   B   OFF   A

INDEX

Numbers in italics refer to captions.

A

Abstract patterns 78, 68, 154
Amateur Photographer 172
Assistant
    duties of 10, 72, *72*, 82, 148

B

Baby oil 84, *84*, 150
Background *see* Settings
Background paper
    colour of 68, *68*
    frame for 100
    model behind 66, *67*
    spray paint and 62, 116
    use of 70, *99*, 100, *100*, *101*, 116
Balcony settings *144*
Barndoor attachment
    catchlight, use with 114
Bathroom settings 146
Beach settings 36, *78*, 96, *96*, 140, 150,
    152, 154
Bedroom settings *58*, 112, *145*, 146, *147*,
    178
Boats
    photographing on 152, *152*
    props on 152, *152*
Body
    photographing parts of 42, 44, *45*, 90,
        100, 142, *142*
    posing *see* Posing, parts of body
Boom arm 106
Budgets 134

C

Calendar session
    client's contribution to 124, 130
    client's requirements *122*, *123*, 166,
        170
    model's preparation for 16, 130, *130*
    organization of 16, 124
    photographer's contribution to 16,
        124, *124*, *125*, 126, 130
Camera 136, 158, *158*
Camera angle *26*, 46, 146
Colour
    red, impact of 22, *22*
    use of 24, 26, 34, 74, 164, 168
Colour casts
    blue 156
    green 138

Commercial pictures 104, *104*
Composition
    colour in 164, 168
    geometrical shapes in 92, *92*, 96
    lighting in 114
    lines in 22, 24, 30, 36, 62, 96, *96*
    model's pose in 68, *93*, 94, *94*, *95*
    natural light in 96
    rules of 88
    weather in 96
Costume
    contribution to eroticism 42, 74, *75*,
        150, 164
    unusual 86, *86*
Cropping *20*, 36, 46, 90, *90*
Customs regulations 128

D

Dawson, Les 170
Daylight
    artificial light and 110, *110*
    atmospheric 96, 140
    changes in 12
    evening *60*, *97*, 132, 154, 184
    morning 132, 154, 184
    window as source of 98, 112, *112*
    see also Shade *and* Sunlight
Depth of field reduction 26
Dry ice 10, *60*, 82, *82*

E

Equipment
    amateur studio and 98, 100
    care of 158, *158*, 159
    customs and 128, *128*
    location shooting and 110, 136, 156
    see also Camera; Flash; Light,
        artificial; Reflectors; *and* Tripod
Eroticism
    baby oil and 84, 150
    background and 76, 82
    costume and 74, *74*, *75*, 150
    danger and 86, *86*
    glamour photography and 8
    props and 30, *31*, 34, 76, *76*
    unexpectedness and 32, *33*, *35*, *38*,
        62, 140
Expenses
    offsetting 134
Exposure
    calculating 42, 112, 156, *156*
    effects of varying 90, *90*, 154

F

Fantasy 18, *19*, 28, *28*, 60, 64, *64*, *65*,
    126, 152
Film
    requirements 118
    test film 118, *118*
Filter
    soft focus 70
    warm-up 66, 148, 156
Flare effect 98
Flash
    bounced 98
    diffused 106, *107*, 112
    fill-in 138, 148
    flashgun 98, 100, 136
    flash head *112*
    flash meter 112
    flash unit 34, 106, *106*, 110
    natural light and 112
    'shower' and 72
Focusing techniques 26, *27*, 146, 150
Forest settings 138, *138*

G

Glamour photographer
    amateur 8, 20, 78, 80, 100
    professional *passim*
Gray, Jon *passim*

H

Hair
    colour of 18, 54
    length of 18, *18*, 54, *54*
Honeycomb attachment
    flash, use with 106
Humour
    calendar shots and 166
    'fat lady' poster and 182
    importance of 76, 170
    props and 80, *81*
    see also Les Dawson

J

Jamaica 12, 176, 178, 184

K

Kitchen settings 76, 146

L

Landscape photography 88
Law 12, 126
Lens hood 98